PULLMAN

PULLMAN

• The Man, the Company, the Historical Park •

KENNETH J. SCHOON

THE
History
PRESS

Published by The History Press
Charleston, SC
www.historypress.com

First published 2021

Manufactured in the United States

ISBN 9781467149860

Library of Congress Control Number: 2021938370

CONTENTS

Contents

PREFACE

I have always enjoyed travel by train. Whenever I need to go into downtown Chicago, my first inclination is to catch the South Shore line in Northwest Indiana and travel in comfort (now that smoking is not allowed on the cars) and not worry about traffic jams.

The first long-distance railroad trip I remember was back in December 1967, my senior year of college, when my two brothers and I took the train from Chicago to Los Angeles in order to go to the Rose Bowl game. In later years, my wife and I have traveled by train to various places, one being to the Henry Ford Museum/Greenfield Village at Dearborn, Michigan. Those trips and others in between allowed us to see American scenery unavailable to passengers on aircraft but did not give us the experience of traveling during railroad's golden age until the year 2016, when we took a trip that included a train ride from San Francisco to Portland on reconditioned Pullman cars. We slept in a Pullman sleeper and spent the day in a domed/dining car. Riding through the Cascade Mountains with the view from and the comfort of that car was spectacular. Our service mirrored what one might have expected in the 1920s: linen tablecloths, a fresh rose, fine food, attentive service. It was a once-in-a-lifetime experience that we'd like to do again.

So, when two years later I was asked to write a small book for the new Pullman National Monument, I was intrigued and delighted. That small book, available at the gift shop on the Pullman grounds, was too small to contain all I wanted to include. Thus this book. The National Monument has much to offer. Enjoy the trip.

ACKNOWLEDGEMENTS

Many thanks to the following for their help in preparing this book: National Monument superintendent Teri Gage, Sue Bennett, Sylvia DeYoung, Paul Myers, Paul Petraitis, Mike Wolski, Joe Szabo, Mike Shymanski and Mike McMahon. They provided and/or verified text and images for this book, and to my patient wife, Peg Schoon, for her suggestions and copy editing.

ERRATA

Unfortunately, much local history material contains errors, and it would be presumptuous to assume that this book has eliminated them all and has no errors of its own. Readers are therefore encouraged to send corrections to the author at kschoon@iun.edu. Please be specific and, if possible, include some way that the author can confirm the correction.

ABBREVIATIONS

The following abbreviations are used in this book:

aka	also known as
B&O	Baltimore and Ohio Railroad
c or ca	circa, about or approximate
HPF	Historic Pullman Foundation

H&B	Haskell & Barker Car Company
KJS	Kenneth J. Schoon (the author)
NPS	National Park Service
NMB	National Mediation Board
PCO	Pullman Civic Organization
RR	railroad
USGS	United States Geological Survey

INTRODUCTION

Downtown
The Pullman Mansion
Chicago
Pullman

Public domain.

Pullman is the name of a man, a company, a town (today a Chicago neighborhood) and a type of railroad sleeping car. The very name brings to mind luxurious accommodations on Pullman cars and identifies the porters who served in those rail cars, as well as the first major railroad strike and near nationwide boycott. The story of this man, his company and his company town encompasses important segments in the history of urban planning, industrial efficiency, labor/management conflict and race and gender relations.

More than 160 years ago, George Mortimer Pullman realized that many railroad passengers would pay extra for comfort. He built luxurious passenger cars with comfortable, private sleeping accommodations and attentive service. He made a fortune.

In 1880, he consolidated his operations by building an attractive town with a modern industrial complex, row homes and apartments for his employees and commercial buildings to serve their needs. Not liking to relinquish control of his products, he, through his company, maintained ownership of the town's housing and commercial buildings, as well as the thousands of Pullman sleeper cars that they made.

1

PULLMAN'S GEOLOGIC BEGINNINGS

The ground at Pullman is today about eleven feet above the average current level of Lake Michigan. But Lake Michigan's water level was originally much higher than today, and what is now Pullman spent thousands of years under the surface of that lake.[1]

Lake Michigan was formed by glacial activities that gouged out the bottom of the lake and then deposited some of that eroded material in terminal moraines that parallel the shoreline of the southern part of the lake. The largest of these is called the Valparaiso Moraine. The high, rolling moraines then trapped the waters from the melting glacier, forming the beginnings of Lake Michigan. At various times since the lake's formation about 14,500 years ago, the lake level has fallen—leaving the Pullman area above water—and then risen, inundating the area again.

Then about 4,700 years ago, the lake level stabilized long enough to form a beach about one half mile west of Pullman—just east of where Michigan Avenue now runs through the community of Roseland. The edge of that ancient shoreline is still visible when one travels west from Pullman on 111th Street.

When the lake level dropped from the Michigan Avenue elevation, it left the former shoreline high above a relatively flat, low and marshy area between it and what later became Lake Calumet—then just a shallow inlet of Lake Michigan. Over the last two thousand years, much of this area, because of weather conditions, fluctuated between being soggy and dry.

The 1870s found this region sparsely inhabited but close to the already prosperous community of Roseland to the west and to the Kensington railroad station development to the south. The area that would become the town of Pullman, then still outside of the city of Chicago, was nicely

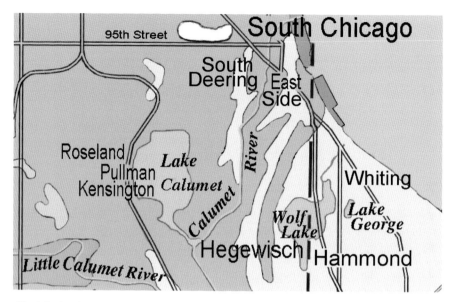

All of the land shown here was under Lake Michigan when the lake was larger five thousand years ago. White areas near the state line indicate the dune and swale topography of the lower Tolleston shorelines, intermediate shades on the left are sand ridges and the dark area surrounding Lake Calumet is lake (Michigan) bottom land with clay-based soils. The small white area at the top is "Stony Island," which was a stone reef similar to, but smaller than, the better-known one at Thornton. *Schoon, 2003.*

sandwiched between the Illinois Central Railroad and Lake Calumet, which was connected via the Calumet River to Lake Michigan. Thus, transportation of goods and people to and from the site by rail or eventually by water would not be a problem.

Before development, much of the land gradually sloped downward toward Lake Calumet, whose shore was much closer to the Pullman area than it is now. Its clay soils were rather impermeable, causing rainwater to pond on the surface of the ground, creating in places a marshy, wet prairie landscape.

In the mid-nineteenth century, wetlands were not appreciated, and draining such areas was called "reclaiming" the land. In their natural state, these lands were considered worthless. They were often too wet to support either agriculture or physical development.

Thus, one of the first things the Pullman company did was to dredge clay from the bottom of Lake Calumet (which was then only a few feet deep) and dump it on what would become the town site, thus raising the ground level of the low areas up to, perhaps, five feet above its natural elevation. With the underground sewers installed by the company, the ground dried out, allowing the plant and residential buildings to be built.

EVOLUTION OF THE PULLMAN AND SURROUNDING AREAS OVER THE YEARS AFTER 1890

Michigan Avenue and the ancient High Tolleston Shoreline are at the far left of each map.
Kensington Station is at the bottom left of each map.
The black rectangles are large buildings.
Note how Lake Calumet has shrunk over the years.

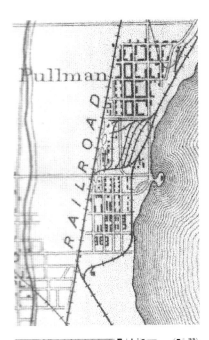
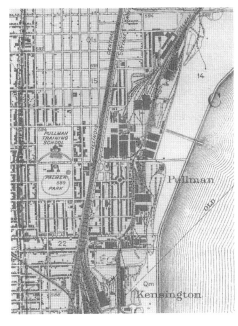

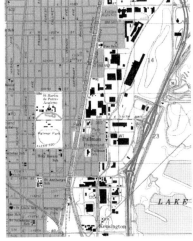

Above, left: **1889**. Though this map has errors in building placement, it does show how close Lake Calumet was then to the town of Pullman. The "island" was the site of Pullman company's boathouse and sporting events. *United States Geological Survey (USGS).*

Above, right: **1937**. White areas next to Lake Calumet are "made land," created by the Pullman company as it needed more space. Roseland west of the IC tracks has been developed. *USGS.*

Left: **1997**. Dark gray areas are city blocks filled with housing. The curving double line is Interstate 94. East of that highway and north of the lake is a Chicago sanitary landfill. Lake Calumet has been deepened and docking facilities built. *USGS.*

15

2

THE RAILROAD ERA BEGINS

America's railroad era began on Christmas Day 1830, sixty-one days before the birth of George Pullman. That day was when the first locomotive fully crafted in the United States began its run in Charleston, South Carolina. The brand-new Charleston and Hamburg Railroad then began the country's first railroad passenger service as it slowly (at twenty-one miles per hour) pulled one freight car and two passenger coaches some six miles to the town of Hamburg, South Carolina. Approximately 140 excited passengers sat on uncushioned wooden benches in these two open-air coaches,[2] which looked more like stagecoaches than modern railroad cars.[3]

Scheduled passenger train service began three years later when then the Camden and Amboy Railroad started running between Bordentown and South Amboy, New Jersey—a trip of only thirty-four miles. The company claimed that in spite of unexpected en route delays such as cattle on the tracks, it could regularly make the trip in less than three hours.[4]

The earliest locomotives used wood for fuel, and as wood burns quickly, they had to stop frequently to refuel. As there wasn't much track laid yet, trips by rail in the earliest days were of short duration. Thus there was no need to worry about eating or sleeping on board. However, new railroad companies were formed, and miles of track began to be laid across the eastern part of North America. As the tracks got longer, so did the trips, and not surprisingly passengers needed food and rest.

Early Sleeping Cars

In 1836, sixteen years before the first railroad from the East even reached Chicago, Pennsylvania's Cumberland Valley Railroad may have been the first line to put beds in its coaches. In any event, the first patent for a sleeping car was issued two years later.[5]

By 1855, newspaper advertisements from several railroad lines promoted "sleepers."[6] These cars had tiers of three bunks on each side of the coach—the lowest near or on the floor. It was said that passengers in a higher bunk might be flung out of bed whenever the train rounded a corner at a good rate of speed.[7] There was no privacy. Men would lie down on the beds fully dressed. Women and children tended to avoid this arrangement and would simply get off the train in the evening and spend the night in a trackside hotel. At daybreak, blankets were piled at the back of the car.[8] As these coaches had beds permanently affixed to their walls, they couldn't be used for daytime travel.

Responding to Hunger and Thirst

At first, railroad managements apparently didn't give much thought to serving food on board; nevertheless, the passengers did get hungry—sometimes even on short runs. Many passengers learned to bring nonperishable food with them. One passenger wrote, "When everybody in the car got out their lunch baskets…it was an interesting sight.…The aroma from those lunches hung around the car all day, and the flies wired ahead for their friends to meet them at each station."

Those less prepared took advantage of eager entrepreneurs who waited for the trains to arrive at various stations for refueling and then sold snacks and sweets to the hungry passengers who disembarked in order to stretch their legs and find something to eat. Because their fuel burned quickly, trains had to stop to refuel frequently, so there were plenty of opportunities for hungry passengers to find something to eat. When the engineer or conductor rang his bell, the passengers would climb back on board and the train would take off.[9]

Unfortunately for the passengers, there were no health standards at the time, and with little or no competition, much of the food for sale was stale. According to railroad historian James Porterfield, these trackside offerings were nearly universally described as being terrible. The breads could be dry, the meats tough and the coffee bitter.

Occasionally, of course, the trains might stop near an inn or home where the travelers were welcome to order dinner. But they had to hurry, as refueling stops seldom exceeded twenty minutes. Some lines allowed vendors to come on board and sell items while the train was in motion, but in doing this, the vendor would have to get off the train and get back to where he started. One of the first "refreshment" services offered by railroad staff were makeshift bars set up in the baggage car, where male passengers could buy drinks.[10]

Visionary entrepreneurs soon were building restaurants right next to the tracks—sometimes renting space in the depots themselves. The staff at these places knew that they needed to serve the passengers efficiently and quickly because they still had only twenty minutes to disembark, find a table, eat and get back onto the train.

Available food service improved when en route conductors started using telegraph services to wire ahead, informing a particular establishment how many of his passengers intended to eat there. That way food was ready to eat when the passengers arrived.[11] They still had a scant twenty minutes to eat before the train got moving again.

As years passed, larger and more elegant hotels and eating establishments were situated along rail routes. And yet the nicer the eating and sleeping establishments were, the more the passengers might want to linger and enjoy a meal. This ran counter to the goals of the railroad companies, whose goals were speed, keeping on schedule and making trips between distant cities faster than their competitors. As the trains were able to run faster, and as efficient coal-burning locomotives could travel farther between refueling stops, trains simply couldn't accommodate the myriad "rest stops" that had been established along their routes. Having lost their rail customers, many of these facilities simply closed their doors for good.

The short-lived Philadelphia, Germantown and Norristown Railroad (1832–1838) ran passenger cars—at that time not much larger than stagecoaches—with a bar and several shelves behind it, which suggests that at least drinks, if not nonperishable foods, were served there. As there was no place set aside for preparation, food was brought aboard before departure or purchased at stops along the way.[12]

The first recorded description of a meal prepared and served on a moving train was in 1842: on a special B&O Railroad excursion, in a separate car, staff prepared an elegant cold luncheon (supervised by a well-known restaurateur) and served it to the railroad's president and directors. The food was excellent but overshadowed by the novelty of enjoying a meal while moving through the countryside at twenty-five miles an hour.[13] It is unknown whether the distinguished passengers ate at tables set up for them or held their lunches in their laps.

For about twenty years, food service on trains was limited to similar special events. Then in 1862, the Philadelphia, Wilmington and Baltimore line had a "refreshment car" designed for eating—with a partition in the center of the car separating the smoking and eating sections. Hot foods were prepared at depots and brought into the car just before departure. An 1863 publication noted, "The experiment of supplying passengers with comfortable meals, including all the delicacies found in first-class hotels has proved a great success."[14]

It was the Civil War and trains carrying wounded soldiers to hospitals that necessitated the actual preparation and serving of food on board. By 1863, several railroad lines had hospital trains with a kitchen car that had cupboards, a sink and a stove near a serving area with a long table and benches. Soldiers who were too ill to eat at this table would have their food carried to boxcars where they would be resting and waiting.

3

GEORGE PULLMAN IN NEW YORK

George Mortimer Pullman grew up in a New York family that made things. Lewis Pullman, his father, was a carpenter in Salem Cross Roads (later called Brockton), New York, the town where George was born on March 3, 1831. Being a skilled carpenter, Mr. Pullman was probably paid the top salary, three dollars a day.[15] Lewis and his wife, Emily, had ten children, two of whom died young. George's two older brothers, Royal Henry and Albert, also became carpenters and later established a cabinetmaking business.[16] In addition to carpentry, George's father found employment moving buildings, a job that often required him to spend time away from home.[17] An inventor as well, in 1841 Lewis patented a machine to make it easier to move them.[18]

In the spring of 1845, fourteen-year-old George, having finished the fourth grade, quit school and went to work at his uncle's store, where he learned a great deal about commerce and merchandising. Later that year, his parents and younger siblings moved to Albion, New York, right on the Erie Canal, so that Lewis could be closer to his work. The three older boys all stayed at Salem Cross Roads.

After three years, the boys joined their parents in Albion. Henry and Albert opened a cabinetmaking shop, and George became an apprentice cabinetmaker. Later, George worked for his father, often serving as the fixer whenever problems arose.[19] So, when Lewis Pullman died in 1853, George, then just twenty-two and the oldest unmarried son, took over his father's moving business, entering into a partnership with a fellow Albion resident, Charles Henry Moore. George cared for his widowed mother, Emily, the rest of her life.

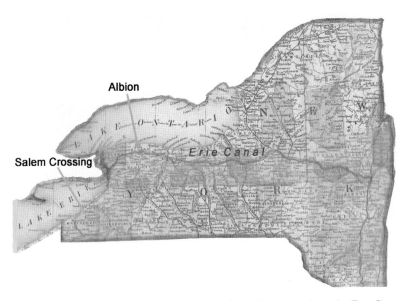

The Erie Canal, darkened for effect, made it easier for settlers to get from the East Coast to the Middle West. *Mitchell, 1865.*

When the State of New York decided to widen the Erie Canal, it contracted with Pullman and Moore to move twenty or more buildings away from the expanded canal right-of-way.[20] For the next six years, they and six to twelve hired men worked on this project six days a week.

At five feet, seven inches tall and 160 pounds, George Pullman was a man of average build, but he looked young for his age.[21] This undoubtedly influenced his decision to grow facial hair, which he kept the rest of his life.

As he worked alongside the canal, George Pullman must have realized that travel by train would soon eclipse travel by canal. Trains were faster and, more importantly, could continue to operate all winter. So, he paid attention when a friend of his, former state senator Benjamin Field, began building sleeping cars for the New York Central Railroad.

Travel by rail at that time was cheaper and faster than other modes of transportation but not at all comfortable.[22] George Pullman once described the three-and-a-half-day trip from New York to Chicago as a "nightmare." Besides being uncomfortable while on the train, there was no one direct route. One then expected to have to change trains at least once, and there might be a long delay at any one station waiting for one's connecting trip.[23] Many travelers did at least plan their trips so that come evening they could disembark and spend the night at a comfortable hotel near the depot.

Not long afterward, on a trip by railroad to Buffalo, George examined one of the train's sleepers. Like other sleepers at that time, it had vertical tiers of three berths—one near the floor with a fee of one dollar, one midway up that cost seventy-five cents and one near the ceiling that cost just fifty cents. He paid the dollar so that he could try out the expensive bed. He was disgusted; the bed was uncomfortable. Not only that, the ceiling was so low that a tall man wouldn't be able to stand up straight. The car was unventilated, and the stoves at each end created a dreadful atmosphere. He didn't sleep but wondered what could be done to make a better experience.[24] Shortly afterward, Pullman formed a sleeping car partnership with Senator Field.[25] But at that time, he didn't have time to devote to this concern.

By coincidence, at some social event George Pullman met Mrs. Joel Matteson, the wife of the owner of the Matteson House Hotel in Chicago. She told him about the need to find some firm that could lift that hotel "out of the mud" and there were many other buildings in Chicago with the same need.[26]

So, when his moving contract with the State of New York ended in 1859—and seeing little hope for much more work in New York—George Pullman applied for and won the contract to raise Chicago's Matteson Hotel. Before moving, however, he ordered one thousand jackscrews to be shipped to Chicago,[27] then the fastest-growing city in the country.[28]

4

RAISING CHICAGO AND
PULLMAN'S FIRST SLEEPERS

In the 1850s, Chicago had serious drainage problems. The downtown area, being quite near the Lake Michigan shore (which was then about where Michigan Avenue is today), was so low in elevation that sewers couldn't effectively drain water into the lake. To solve the problem, the city had to be lifted up to a higher elevation. The main business street at that time was Lake Street.

Twenty-eight-year-old George Pullman arrived in Chicago in the spring of 1859. With his experience in moving buildings and running a business, and with a contract to raise the Matteson Hotel downtown at the intersection of Randolph and Dearborn Streets, he was undoubtedly anxious to get started. The hotel was a prestigious building in the city, second only to the Tremont House Hotel. He was given forty-eight days for his crew to raise the hotel five feet; with eight hundred jackscrews under the building, the job was completed in ten days.[29]

Specific Methods Were Used to Raise Building

Buildings were lifted with jacks as automobiles can be today. In this case, workers would dig holes near a building's foundation and insert strong timbers and jackscrews. Large buildings required thousands of jackscrews. When the foreman (George Pullman himself on many occasions) blew a whistle, workers would all simultaneously rotate the screws a quarter turn. As the building rose, additional timbers would be inserted on top of the timbers already there to hold the building at its new level, while other workmen installed new footings. The process would be repeated over and over until the building was at the desired height.

Right: George Pullman, circa 1861. *Courtesy of Pullman State Historic Site.*

Below: Raising a block of buildings on Lake Street, Chicago. *Edward Mendel, 1860.*

Many other jobs followed that one, including one in May 1860, that, teamed with two other firms, lifted an entire city block at once. George Pullman and the other contractors were so pleased with the process that they commissioned a lithograph to be made by Edward Mendel illustrating the process.[30]

His firm's biggest challenge came in 1861, when it, along with others, was hired to raise by six or seven feet the largest building in town: the massive brick six-story Tremont House Hotel. That feat was amazingly accomplished with the hotel employees and guests remaining inside.[31] Although George Pullman is usually given credit for this accomplishment, the honor truly should go to his brother Albert, who supervised the work, as George was in Colorado at the time.[32]

Being busy with raising buildings did not stop George Pullman from pursuing his other interest in sleeping accommodations on railroad cars. As he believed that there were many well-to-do and business travelers who would pay extra for extra comfort, George Pullman's sleeping cars would be designed for elegance and comfort.

So, not forgetting his own belief that he could design more comfortable sleeping cars, George Pullman found time to suggest to managers of the Chicago, Alton and St. Louis Railroad that he could design for them a practical sleeping car—one more comfortable than what was then available. The biggest problem at the time, besides comfort, was arranging for nighttime sleep in the same car that was used for daytime travel.

Intrigued by his suggestions, the railroad company gave him permission to alter two of its passenger cars. Over the summer of 1859, George Pullman supervised the gutting and rebuilding of their interiors. The remodeled cars had cherrywood interiors and plush upholstery. They each had four upper and four lower berths with small lavatories at both ends of each car. During the day, the upper berths were kept at the top of the car. At night, an attendant would first lower the backs of the plush and comfortable seats until they were horizontal and then lower the upper berths halfway to the floor. He would then provide a mattress and blanket for each passenger. Curtains provided some privacy. The Chicago, Alton and St. Louis managers were so pleased with the new sleepers that they ordered an additional six cars. The Field & Pullman firm acquired another customer when the Galena and Chicago Union Railroad ordered some cars.

The remodeled cars went into use in August of that year and were soon recognized as a superior way to travel on overnight trips. Yet in spite of their good intentions, the first two cars built by Field & Pullman were, by later standards, still quite primitive. The upper berths actually hung from the ceiling. In the morning, they were raised back to the top of the car with ropes and pulleys. Many years later, Robert Bartsch, a retired Pullman employee, noted that folks who used the tiny washroom had to use a hand pump in order to get water in the basin and that there was no hot water at

The interior of car "Number 9," 1859, Pullman's first attempt of combining day travel with comfortable sleeping. The upper berths are attached to the ceiling. *Leydendecker.*

all. And the toilet: "Well—" he said, "the less said about it the better. But all in all, it conformed to the sanitary code of the day."[33]

J.L. Barnes, who was the porter for the first-ever trip of Pullman's sleeper, remembered that on the first night he had to "compel the passengers to take their boots off before they got into the berths. They…seemed afraid to take them off."[34] Unfortunately for Barnes, after a few trips, the railroad executives decided that a porter was not necessary, and he lost his job. The train's conductor then was assigned to the sleeping car as well as the rest of the train.[35]

However, within one year after his arrival in Chicago, George Pullman's building raising and sleeping car redesigning businesses were doing well, and he was becoming a well-known young Chicago businessman.[36]

5

GOLD FEVER

THE COLORADO GOLD RUSH

The Colorado or Pike's Peak gold rush started in 1859, about ten years after the more famous California gold rush. The excitement in the country caused by reports of gold in the Rocky Mountains resulted in about 100,000 prospectors pouring into the area. Although first known as the "Pike's Peak" gold rush, the location of the gold, and therefore the gold mining camps, was about eighty-five miles north of Pike's Peak in what was then the western part of Kansas Territory. The sudden increase in population resulted in Congress creating the Colorado Territory in February 1861. Colorado would not be admitted to the Union as a state until 1876.

Unfortunately, the Rocky Mountain gold, unlike much found in California, was not found in loose nuggets but rather a visible component in rocks. This rock had to be smashed in order to separate the gold from the quartz and other minerals in the rock. "Stamping" (or crushing) mills could efficiently do that work.

At this point in George Pullman's life, he may not have considered a career in making railroad sleeping cars. The same year (1859) he arrived in Chicago, he caught gold fever and started making plans to head out to Colorado—not to hunt for gold but to supply the needs of prospectors. He realized that he could make money providing meals and sleeping accommodations, supplies and fresh horses for the men heading into the gold fields. Pullman assumed that many prospectors would eventually go home empty-handed, and he wanted better results than that. Just as he had in New York and Chicago, while he was out west, George Pullman formed

George Pullman in Colorado, *after* having a shave. *Colorado Historical Society.*

partnerships with other men in order to begin to operate his various businesses there.

Before leaving for the gold fields, he ordered a stamping mill from the Eagle Iron Works and had it delivered to Denver.

In June 1860, George Pullman boarded a Pullman car (of course) on the Chicago, Alton and St. Louis Railroad and headed to St. Louis.[37] Two days later, he took the North Missouri Railroad approximately three hundred miles northwest to St. Joseph, Missouri, just across the river from the Kansas Territory. Then, he boarded a stagecoach for the five-to-eight-mile-an-hour, six-hundred-mile, seven-day trip to Denver.[38] No doubt, he compared the lack of comfort on this trip to the much more pleasant accommodations he was at that time providing for rail passengers on his "Pullman" cars back in Chicago.

Life out west was much different than it was in Chicago. The Tremont House (named for the Chicago hotel) was just a log cabin that didn't yet have any doors or windows. On occasion, Pullman spent the night sleeping on a pile of hay with a rolled-up coat as his pillow. The differences in life were, naturally, reflected in the clothes that he wore. Back home he dressed conservatively, but in a way that identified him as a man of means. Out west, as he described in a letter to his mother, he became a "rough-looking subject,"[39] sporting a gray flannel shirt and gray pants that he tucked into his boots and didn't shave regularly. On Sundays, he'd relent and wear a white shirt.

While on his stagecoach ride, George Pullman met James Lyon, and they decided to work together under the name Lyon, Pullman & Company. After several days of walking around the area, they selected a place in Russell Gulch to construct a building for their mill, which by then had arrived. Having customers right away, they hired fifteen men and six yokes of cattle to power their mill. Fairly successful, the mill ran day and night, six days a week, and produced $5,000 worth of gold in its first seven weeks.

The Pullman complex consisted of two cabins: one for his mill, the other for himself, his housekeeper Mrs. Scott, her husband and several workers at the mill. The rough-hewn dining table could seat sixteen people for meals and then serve as a bed for two of them at night. Mrs. Scott cooked meals on a little stove that was kept outside the front door. By October, he had enlarged both buildings; his "house" then included two private bedrooms with real beds. His room was carpeted with gunnysacks.[40]

Also in the fall of 1860, Lyon and Pullman purchased land in nearby Central City for their general store. On November 11, a wagon train that they had commissioned consisting of twenty-six or twenty-eight wagons pulled by one hundred yokes of oxen arrived with groceries and dry goods for their store. They moved all the goods into the building and opened the store to customers on December 6.

It was never George Pullman's desire to hunt for gold, rather he went out west to sell food, provisions and services to those who were doing the mining. In what became a routine, he usually spent three hours every morning checking his receipts and expenses, making business calls and checking in at the mill. Every few weeks, he would travel to Denver, and once a month he'd check up on his haying business. Later he would ride over to the store, where he did whatever needed to be done that day until 3:00 p.m., when the mail arrived.[41] Mining, of course, had to shut down when the nearby grounds were covered with snow.

By the end of the year, George Pullman and his partners were running several stamping mills, at least two general stores and a sawmill while dealing in gold dust and investing in some mining operations and hay fields so that horses would have enough feed to get through the winter.[42] In addition, the firm purchased a ranch near the town of Golden, the capital of the new Colorado Territory. He had hoped to go home for Christmas but found himself too involved in his business ventures to afford the time away.[43]

In June 1861, George Pullman got his Colorado affairs in order and headed back to Chicago to see to his businesses there. However, by the spring of 1862, he felt he had to return to Colorado. Once there, he realized that his partner, James Lyon, was more of a speculator than Pullman thought wise, and their books showed some discrepancies. Lyon wasn't dishonest in any way, just a little more carefree than was appreciated. Pullman didn't stay out west long this time and by July headed back to Chicago. Six months later, he was back in Colorado—this time for the last time.

George Pullman came to realize that it was extremely difficult to manage businesses in such distant parts of the country. His mother and siblings were in Chicago and somewhat unreliable partners in Colorado. He was familiar with the intricacies of promotion and marketing and less so with mining, an industry that could die a quick death when the available gold ran out. He probably made little money from his mining operations, but perhaps as much as $100,000 from merchandising operations. The travel between the two locations was difficult at best. And besides, he still wanted to design sleeping cars for more railroad lines. He decided to end his Wild West adventure.

In April 1863, George Pullman returned to Chicago, wealthier than he was when he first headed west. In later years, he would occasionally return to visit his old acquaintances in Colorado, who were always glad to see him.

While he was out west, the Civil War had changed the pace of life in Chicago. There was more prosperity, as Chicagoans won contracts to supply the Union army with meat and supplies while railroad lines were busy moving soldiers to where they were needed. The city grew, and business was good.

Employing a legal policy at the time, George Pullman was able to avoid serving in the Union army by hiring a man to take his place.[44]

6

IMPROVING THE SLEEPER CAR

B ecause Field & Pullman was not the only company making sleeping cars, George Pullman evidently decided that the only way to succeed would be to design and make cars so luxurious that they would be the only sleepers that wealthy passengers would deem suitable. As he had made many uncomfortable trips, he still believed that there were many well-to-do and business travelers who would gladly pay a higher fee for extra comfort. Consequently, George Pullman's sleeping cars would be designed for elegance and comfort.

In 1863, the Field & Pullman Company designed its largest, most attractive sleeper yet, a fifty-six-passenger, fifty-eight-foot-long parlor/sleeping car made by a company in Springfield, Massachusetts. Named the *Springfield*, it had a spacious private stateroom at each end of the car with a writing table, a bed with a first-class mattress and clean sheets that, like a hotel, were changed every day.[45] The center section of the car had sofas for daytime use that converted into beds at night. Over the beds were bunks that folded down from the ceiling.

The next year (1864), Field & Pullman built its own car for the first time. Leasing space from the Chicago & Alton line (where Union Station is today), the forty-eight-passenger *Pioneer* was George Pullman's first "truly grand"[46] sleeping car. It was two feet higher and a foot wider than what was then the industry standard, more spacious than any car yet built.

The *Pioneer*'s interior was magnificent, called "the wonder of the age."[47] It boasted brocaded fabric, the finest bed linens (changed daily), highly

The *Pioneer*, larger and more spacious than standard passenger cars. Twenty-nine years after it was built, it was displayed at the Chicago World's Fair in 1893 as shown here. *Courtesy of Pullman State Historic Site.*

polished wooden door frames, an elegant carpet that softened one's steps, a hand-painted mural ceiling, marble-topped washbasins and gilt-edged mirrors that reflected sunlight in the day and the silver coal lamps at night.[48] The car had twelve luxury compartments and high clerestory windows so that natural sunlight brightened the car's center all day long. Curtains, when drawn, provided privacy for the fifty-two passengers that could be accommodated at night. They turned the berths into private compartments, each of which had its own mirrors and lights.[49] Heat was provided by a furnace located under the car (rather than wood stoves at each end).[50]

Although the car was luxurious, it was so expensive that no railroads would buy it. It cost $18,000* at a time when other, less elegant cars sold for $4,000.[51] So Field & Pullman decided to lease their cars to the various railroad lines and provide staff to serve each of them.[52] Even with a great deal of publicity, there were still no takers.

Finally, after months of the cars sitting idle, the Michigan Central Railroad agreed to use them in a one-month trial period. Pullman quickly commissioned four additional cars. But because the Michigan Central would have to charge passengers more to sleep on this new type of car, the Michigan Central insisted that each new "Field/Pullman" car have a cheaper old sleeper car just behind it. Passengers could then choose to either pay fifty to seventy-five cents to sleep on the old cars or pay a whopping two dollars for space in one of the Pullman cars. The trial was successful. The old cars were deserted. Comfort and luxury won.[53]

---

* In 1864, $18,000 could purchase a modest home plus horse and carriage.

A number of historic documents have stated that in May 1865, the *Pioneer* was used on the train that carried President Abraham Lincoln's body from Chicago to Springfield, but none of the accounts was written at the time of Lincoln's funeral. It is known that Colonel James H. Bowen headed the Chicago committee planning for the Lincoln funeral train's arrival in Chicago and its subsequent travel to Springfield. Perhaps Bowen selected the *Pioneer* to be part of the train carrying the casket on its final journey from Chicago to Springfield. This trip then added to the *Pioneer's* fame and thus was responsible for an increase in Field & Pullman's sales.

There is a rather common misconception that George Pullman invented or at least designed the first railroad sleeping car. This is not true. When he was working in Chicago, companies back east were building sleeping cars. As Field and Pullman designed and built their cars, they had to be careful not to infringe on their competitors' patented designs.[54] Their goal remained constant: to make their cars so elegant that passengers would not want to travel on any other company's car.

Sleeping car interior, circa 1870s. *Courtesy of Pullman State Historic Site.*

The company's next major creation was called *The President*, a two-car set in which one car was a luxury sleeper and the other a dining car and kitchen; together they were basically a hotel on wheels. In order to attract high-paying customers, *The President* served exquisite meals and had impeccable service that, it was said, "rivaled the finest hotels of the day."[55]

The Pullman hotel cars carried 133 different food items, a wine chest, ice chest, cloth napkins and fine tablecloths, plus all the china, glassware and utensils that would be needed between departure and the next stop, where more supplies could be loaded.[56] Before it was time to eat, a conductor would walk through the car taking food orders from the passengers. The menu included six hot dishes, four types of cold meat, five different types of bread and a variety of in-season fruits and vegetables. Then a small table would be brought in, placed in front of each seat and, for stability, affixed to the side of the car.

One satisfied passenger noted that his experience on a Pullman hotel car was so grand that royalty would not be "more comfortably housed than the occupant of a Pullman, provided the car be a hotel one."[57] This traveler also noted that passengers on the non-Pullman cars in that train had to, as soon as the train stopped for refueling, rush off the train in order to purchase something to eat and then quickly swallow the likely ill-cooked foods.[58]

Customers liked the Field & Pullman cars, and by December 1866, there were forty-eight of them running along midwestern rails,[59] including every major line connecting with Chicago.[60]

7

THE PULLMAN PALACE CAR COMPANY

In 1867, when Senator Field withdrew from their partnership, George Pullman enlisted new investors and took advantage of Illinois's new incorporation laws by incorporating the new firm as the "Pullman Palace Car Company." George maintained 50 percent of the stock, and as expected, he was made president and general manager, which included the all-important marketing aspects of the company, while his older brother Albert, an experienced cabinetmaker, became the overseer of manufacturing. It was George's job to convince railroad administrators that his sleepers, in spite of being more expensive, were worth the expense because their use would increase ridership.

In March of that year, the new company produced its first luxurious "drawing room" or parlor car, a car where passengers, for an extra fee, could spend the day in a comfortable chair, similar to what one would find in one's own drawing room (today a living room). A major difference was that these chairs swiveled so that one could face any direction one chose. These cars particularly exemplified the company's new name, Palace Car Company.

On June 13, George Pullman married Harriett Sanger, daughter of the owner of a Chicago construction company. Over the next eight years, they had four children: Florence, Harriet and twins George Jr. and Walter Sanger (commonly known as Sanger). During that time, Pullman sleeping cars became increasingly popular with the traveling public, and more and more railroads put in orders for them.

A parlor car equipped with swivel easy chairs. *Courtesy of Pullman State Historic Site.*

A Pullman dining car on the Chicago and Alton Railroad, circa 1900. *Petraitis collection.*

In 1868, the company unveiled its new car, the *Delmonico*, a sixty-foot-long stand-alone dining car named after a well-known New York restaurant. Service on this car was first-class: gourmet dinners served on tables with linen tablecloths, fine china and silver. Meals were prepared by two cooks in a custom-built eight-foot-square kitchen and served by waiters in starched white jackets.[61] At night, the seats were converted into bunks for the staff.[62]

Skilled Pullman workers painting the gold trim on the sleeping car Atlantic at the Detroit plant, circa 1870s. *Courtesy of Pullman State Historic Site.*

Unfortunately, the dining car did not pay for itself. At this time, dining cars on trains were not common. It wasn't until the 1880s that they became a standard part of long-distance train rides.

By 1869, with workshops in several different communities, including one in Ontario, the company boasted seventy cars in service. But the next year that total doubled, as Pennsylvania Railroad started using Pullman sleeping cars for its entire nationwide fleet.[63]

To eliminate some of its competition and be able to take advantage of patents it did not own, the Pullman company began purchasing and absorbing competing companies.[64] During this time, in order to keep up with demand, many Pullman cars were being built on contract by other companies. As even more orders arrived, and in order to consolidate all of his plants in one location, George Pullman bought the Detroit Car and Manufacturing Company and for a decade built all of his cars in Detroit.[65]

The company would have dearly loved to provide sleepers for the big eastern rail lines, but two other manufacturing companies, both with strong backing, dominated that market: the Wagner Car Company, run by Commodore Cornelius Vanderbilt (purchased by the Pullman company in 1899, two years after George Pullman's death), and Pullman's biggest competitor,[66] the Central Transportation Company, which was partially owned[67] but controlled[68] by Andrew Carnegie.

The following story was published by Dale Carnegie (no relation to Andrew) in his best seller *How to Win Friends and Influence People*:

> The Central Transportation Company, which Andrew Carnegie controlled, was fighting with the company that Pullman owned. Both were struggling to get the sleeping-car business of the Union Pacific Railroad, bucking each other, slashing prices, and destroying all chance of profit. Both Carnegie and Pullman had gone to New York to see the board of directors of the Union Pacific.
>
> Meeting one evening [in 1870][69] in the St. Nicholas Hotel, Carnegie said: "Good evening, Mr. Pullman, aren't we making a couple of fools of ourselves?" "What do you mean?" Pullman demanded.
>
> Then Carnegie expressed what he had on his mind—a merger of their two interests. He pictured in glowing terms the mutual advantages of working with, instead of against, each other.
>
> Pullman listened attentively, but he was not wholly convinced. Finally he asked, "What would you call the new company?" and Carnegie replied promptly: "Why, the Pullman Palace Car Company, of course." Pullman's face brightened. "Come into my room," he said. "Let's talk it over."

That talk made railroad history.[70] The Pullman Palace Car Company kept its name, and George Pullman ended up owning all of Central's patents.

The next year (1871), George Pullman and Andrew Carnegie, along with a few others, bailed out the Union Pacific Railroad, which was having serious financial difficulties. Both men then got themselves elected to the

The Pullman family residence at 1729 Prairie Avenue in Chicago. *Petraitis collection.*

company's board of directors, and the Union Pacific started using Pullman sleeping cars.[71]

The Pullmans survived the great Chicago Fire of 1871, and fortunately George had time to save important papers before his offices were consumed by flames. For two years, while running his company, he served as treasurer of the Chicago Relief and Aid Society helping those who were less fortunate.[72]

Like many wealthy families, the Pullmans had a large summer home. Theirs was in Long Branch, New Jersey. On their first trip there in 1871, they stayed a few days with President Ulysses S. Grant and his family.[73] Of course, whenever they went, they took the train, which included several private cars for the family, their luggage, twelve servants, three vehicles and five horses.[74] Once a year, the extended Pullman family trekked up to the Thousand Islands region of upstate New York, where they had purchased one of the islands and built several cabins. They usually arrived there in time for Emily Pullman's August 14 birthday.

But Pullman still had serious competition. In 1875, Commodore Vanderbilt had the Michigan Central line replace its Pullman cars with Wagner Company sleepers, leaving Pullman without any line going to New

York City. In response, George Pullman helped create a new rail route from Chicago to New York with trains carrying his Pullman cars. In short time, this new route was carrying more passengers than the Michigan Central. Newspapers reporting on this credited the success to the public wanting to travel on Pullman cars.[75] George was pleased.

As a wealthy man and president of a grand and growing company, George Pullman felt that he needed a grand residence in Chicago for his growing family and their guests. Consequently, in 1877, the Pullmans had a massive three-story, mansard-roofed, greystone mansion built on Chicago's fashionable south Prairie Avenue. Besides its elegantly appointed rooms, the house contained a bowling alley and a billiard room.[76] Its grounds contained a beautiful garden with lighted fountains, a domed conservatory[77] and stables. It was said to be the most impressive home on the avenue.[78]

A religious and civic-minded citizen, George regularly worshipped at Chicago's St. Paul's Universalist Church, often attending both morning and evening services. He was a member, and frequently an officer, not only of the Chicago Relief and Aid Society but also the Chicago Citizens' League, the Commercial Club, the Chicago Athenaeum and the Chicago Musical Festival Association.[79] In 1872, he helped found the Chicago YMCA and served as one of the first presidents of its board of directors.[80]

Besides its sleepers, the Pullman Palace Car Company also manufactured parlor (drawing room), dining, mail, baggage, coal, smoking and buffet cars,[81] boxcars, refrigerated cars and streetcars.

By 1879, the company was leasing 464 sleeping cars and netting an annual profit of nearly $1 million.[82] Although the Pullman company is remembered for its sleeping cars, it made far more regular passenger cars than sleepers. Freight cars could be made even quicker and were more profitable than passenger cars. But the big profits came from operating the sleepers.

8

PULLMAN PORTERS AND MAIDS

P art of the charm of traveling in a Pullman sleeper was not just its comfort but its appearance and service. George Pullman's goal was that the passengers in his cars have a most pleasurable experience when awake as well as when asleep. To him, this meant that the cars needed to look luxurious; the eating experience must be as grand as that in the finest restaurants, and even more important, each passenger had to be treated like royalty. Porters would have to be hired to see to the needs of their passengers. He knew that wealthy families were already accustomed to servants, but such a service would be novel and appealing to the middle class.

Consequently, part of the charm of staying in a Pullman sleeping car was to be treated the same as wealthy passengers. As soon as Pullman decided to provide this service for all his passengers, his advertisements for Pullman sleepers began featuring Pullman porters.[83] At least at the beginning, they were one of the features that most clearly put Pullman sleeping cars in a class above the competition.

But the only way George Pullman could ensure the highest level of service, no matter which railroad line passengers were traveling on, would be if his company hired the service employees, trained, evaluated and paid them. As a result, when a company leased Pullman cars, with the cars came their own Pullman-trained porters who would prepare the staterooms and make up the beds before the passengers arrived, making sure that the room was clean and provided with the proper towels, welcome the passengers as they

Pullman porters with their conductor in front of a Pullman dining car. Note the two waiters in the windows. *Michael Bible.*

arrived at a railroad station and tend to their needs (such as polishing their shoes, serving food and drinks and keeping the cars tidy) during their trip. They also ensured that the rooms were well heated, but not too hot, and that all the lighting fixtures worked.[84]

If George Pullman wondered where he could find men who knew how to be polite while subservient, who would work long hours for low wages and who would be unlikely to quit and find better-paying jobs elsewhere, he didn't worry about this very long. With the Civil War over, there was a large number of recently emancipated African American men in the South who met these requirements, many of whom had worked in the great houses of wealthy southerners.[85]

The Pullman Palace Car Company hired Black men to serve as porters from the beginnings of the company in 1867.[86] In years to come, the Pullman Palace Car Company became the largest employer of African American men in the country.[87] Pullman porters, however, were supervised by Pullman conductors, all of whom were white.

Historian Timuel Black described the porters as "good looking, clean and immaculate in their dress; their style was quite manly; their language was very carefully crafted, so that they had a sense of intelligence about them…. They were good role models for young men."[88]

Porters were required to be clean-shaven grammar school (later high school) graduates. Applicants had to submit a photograph; they were the only Pullman applicants to have this requirement. Historian Melinda Chateauvert noted that it was "union lore" that the photo was used to ensure that the applicant's skin color was sufficiently dark so that he would immediately be recognized as a servant.[89] Black women were hired to work as maids on the more expensive cars. They would help ladies with their baths, fix their hair and give manicures. They could also babysit and feed the children. Their numbers were never large. In 1926, with ten thousand porters working for Pullman, there were only about two hundred maids.[90]

> *The porter was servant as well as host.*
> *He had the best job in his community and the worst on the train.*
> —*Thomas Fleming*, Reflections on Black History

These men practically became the stereotype of the Black servant class and had to silently take a lot of abuse. It became common for passengers to call every porter "George," a disliked moniker that harkened back to a practice of enslaved men using their enslaver's name. But they were trained

Left: A porter gathers shoes to shine before retiring for the night. *Right*: A porter prepares an upper berth. *Library of Congress*.

This 1952 ad featured well-known thrice Academy Award nominee for best actress Gloria Swanson. *Courtesy of Pullman State Historic Site.*

to outwardly accept it. It wasn't until 1926 that the company finally agreed not to discipline porters for ignoring passengers who addressed them as "George" or "boy."[91]

An article in the *Chicago Defender* on December 31, 1910, described the plight of these hardworking men:

> *They spend many days from home and often in places where they are obliged to go hungry....They live on a salary of less than any laboring man, but have families and children to support, which expenses must be met by the incidental tips from public travelers.*[92]

Although their salaries were low, they did receive tips, which they needed. However, they had to work long hours, smile and be pleasant even when they didn't feel like it and sometimes had just four hours of sleep a night—and that on couches in the train's smoking car.

The porters had to purchase their own uniforms, pay for their own meals aboard the train and even pay for the shoe polish that they used for passengers' shoes.[93] They didn't get paid for the time they spent preparing rooms before the arrival of passengers, and when passengers stole Pullman towels, the porters had the cost of replacement towels deducted from their wages.[94]

On the positive side, Pullman porters had a steady income, were required to do little in the way of heavy labor and had the opportunity to see more of America than most Americans ever would. It was, in many cases, the first paying job the porter ever had. The men were respected, considered role models and had high status in their home communities.

Maids were paid less than the porters and had to pay for their uniforms and materials for manicures, as well as their meals.[95] While aboard the trains, neither porters nor maids were allowed to have social conversations with other employees, play cards, smoke, chew gum, drink liquor or swear.[96]

Pullman porters and, on occasion, Hollywood film stars were often featured in the magazine ads that the Pullman Company ran in the first half of the twentieth century.

9

WEST OF LAKE CALUMET
BEFORE PULLMAN

T he Pullman Palace Car Company had trouble keeping up with demand, as its shops in Detroit could only produce 114 cars each year.[97] Thus George Pullman decided that he needed a larger production facility, one that was preferably closer to the railroad lines that were purchasing or would be purchasing his products. He decided that in order to build railroad cars to his exact standards while efficiently keeping up with demand, this new plant would be best located in or near Chicago.

WEST OF LAKE CALUMET, 1862

Fourteen miles south of Chicago's city center (Chicago being then significantly smaller than now) was a rather undeveloped area immediately west of Lake Calumet. Although "empty," it had good transportation potential: the Illinois Central Railroad passed through it, and Lake Calumet was connected to Lake Michigan via the Calumet River. The main thoroughfare through the area was the Michigan City Road, an ancient Indian trail that was west of the Illinois Central tracks.

The land was in Hyde Park Township,* which was much larger in area than the city of Chicago was at that time, extending from what is now 39th

---

* Not to be confused with today's neighborhood called Hyde Park, which predated the township. That community was originally a "suburb" of Chicago, and when the township was created, it took the name of that already existing community.

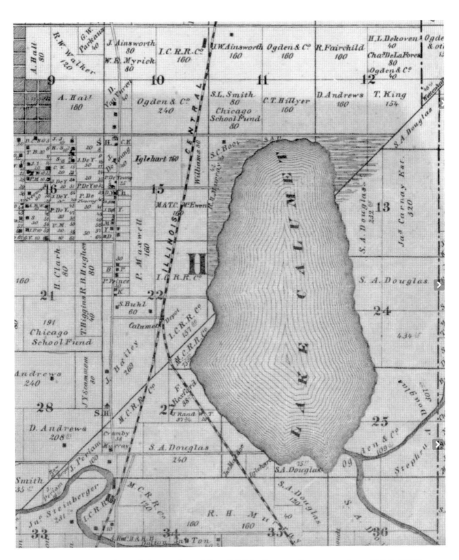

Roseland, unnamed here, is in sections 15 and 16 in the northwest portion of this 1862 map. Pullman would later be built where the large letter H is. *Map of Cook County, Illinois, Burhans & Van Vechten, 1862.*

Street on the north to 138th Street on the south and from State Street on the west to Lake Michigan and the Illinois-Indiana state line on the east.

Although much of the land was either farm or marshland, there were two established communities already in existence—west of the Illinois Central tracks.

ROSELAND, ESTABLISHED 1849

Roseland was the older of the two communities. It was settled in 1849 by fifteen families from the Netherlands who purchased two hundred acres of open land along the Michigan City Road.[98] Their settlement extended along the high ground just west of the High Tolleston Shoreline. (That ancient shoreline of Lake Michigan formed thousands of years ago when Lake Michigan was about twenty-five feet higher than it is now.)

These new arrivals called their settlement (between what are now 103rd and 111th Streets) High Prairie in contrast to the also-Dutch South Holland community, which was called Low Prairie. The Michigan City Road was renamed Michigan Road and is today known as Michigan Avenue. It extended south and passed through Thornton Township along what is still today called the Michigan City Road. The old Indian trail was not a straight line, and neither is the Michigan Avenue of today.

High Prairie soon became the main settlement between the city of Chicago and Indiana.[99] A post office named Hope was established there in 1860, but its name was soon changed to Roseland. It was officially platted as Roseland in 1873. The little village developed a commercial area along Michigan Road, and soon Hyde Park township offices were set up there. Many of the Dutch settlers purchased enough land to establish small truck farms, raising enough food for their families and some to sell for income.

Much of the undeveloped land east of the Tolleston beach ridge was purchased by George Pullman in the late 1870s. In 1884, just as the building of Pullman town was about complete, historian Alfred Andreas wrote that from the village of Roseland up on its high beach ridge "a magnificent view can be had of the palace-car city."[100] In later years, many Pullman employees purchased homes and established churches in Roseland.

KENSINGTON, ESTABLISHED 1852

Kensington, west of the Illinois Central tracks, originally called Calumet Junction, was just that. It got its start in 1852 when two of the earliest rail lines to reach Chicago, the Illinois Central from the South and the Michigan Central from the east, connected and ran one set of tracks, used by both lines, north to the still rather small city of Chicago. Most of the early Kensington residents worked either for the railroads or for the local Chicago

The second Kensington station, circa 1890. *Courtesy of Pullman State Historic Site.*

Forging Company. A post office was established in 1864, but the town grew slowly until 1880.

Everything changed when George Pullman announced that the Pullman Car Works and town would be built east of the tracks, just northeast of Kensington. Boardinghouses were built for the construction crews. That was soon followed by billiard halls and stores selling groceries and other things that their mainly male customers would want.

When it became known that Pullman would have no taverns, a whopping twenty-three taverns opened up in Kensington. Pullman workers couldn't buy a beer in Pullman, but Kensington taverns delivered it across the tracks to grateful Pullman residents. Despite the fact that Kensington also had churches, schools and retail stores, Kensington became known for its taverns. According to the *Encyclopedia of Chicago*, the Dutch in Roseland began referring to Kensington as "Bumtown."[101]

Pullman, which had twelve thousand residents at its peak in 1893, continued to have a great effect on Kensington. The hamlet had just four hundred residents in 1880, the year that ground was broken to build the town of Pullman. Nine years later, Kensington had one thousand residents.[102] Some Kensington residents worked for Pullman, and some Pullman residents worked in Kensington. In 1894, during the Pullman strike, the Kensington German American–owned Turnverein* served as the strike headquarters.

Unfortunately, you won't find Kensington on a Chicago neighborhoods map today. In later years, Roseland's business district along Michigan

---

* Turnvereins were buildings for social gatherings and gymnastics classes built by German immigrants.

Downtown Kensington after the rain. *Petraitis collection.*

Avenue expanded southward into Kensington, obliterating any obvious boundary between the two communities. Later, when sociologists from the University of Chicago divided the city of Chicago into seventy-seven named neighborhoods, Kensington wasn't included. The community was placed in the West Pullman neighborhood.

PULLMAN, ESTABLISHED 1880

The land east of the Illinois Central tracks was less desirable because, being slightly lower than the land farther west, it was in many places simply too wet. Although George Pullman purchased about four thousand acres of land in the township, he decided to build his town in the less desirable six hundred acres between the Illinois Central tracks and Lake Calumet. His advisors knew how to make that happen.

10

PULLMAN

Industrial and Commercial Assets

L ike any employer, George Pullman wanted hardworking, loyal, healthy, dependable and skilled employees. Thus, when he decided to build new shops, his plan was to also build a town that itself might entice the best-qualified people to work for him. By providing more pleasant, well-built brick housing than what was available in nearby Chicago and having many convenient stores and athletic facilities within walking distance, he expected that employees would be happier, more productive and loyal. Coming on the heels of the violent Great Railroad Strike of 1877, during which rail yards in several Illinois cities had been damaged and shut down, George Pullman believed he could design a system that would prevent the labor unrest that caused that earlier conflict.[103] To let the world know what he was planning, he placed advertisements in newspapers locally and abroad.

To him, the Chicago area was the logical choice of location because Chicago was already the midwestern hub of the rapidly expanding railroad industry.[104] The Lake Calumet area, being then outside the city limits, was not subject to either Chicago taxes or control. Just as important to him, his town would be distant from the corruption and "baneful" influences of urban life.[105] When in 1893 a streetcar line was being run south from downtown Chicago to Roseland, George Pullman chose to connect his company town's streetcar line at 95th Street and Stony Island Avenue instead. As long as he kept that land empty, there would be less competition for his housing and for the merchants who had rented retail spaces in his town.

In 1879–80, to avoid last-minute surges in land prices, the company secretly purchased seventy-five parcels[106] of land totaling about four thousand acres.[107] The land was situated fourteen miles south of downtown Chicago in Hyde Park Township just west of Lake Calumet, east of the Roseland Community and northeast of the Illinois Central Railroad's Kensington station. As four thousand acres was far more than he needed for his town and plant complex, much of the arable land was rented to farmers whose produce could be sold both to his employees in Pullman and to the growing markets in Chicago.[108] Much of it was sold piecemeal[109] in later years for a great deal more than what he paid to purchase it.

Much of the Pullman area before development was in agriculture, some of it a marsh, wet much of most years. In the 1870s, it had low value. Not surprisingly, it was largely uninhabited. But the presence of the lake and the Illinois Central Railroad meant that transportation of goods and peoples to and from the site by water or rail would not be a problem. To solve the drainage problem in the lower areas, clay was excavated from the bottom of Lake Calumet and spread over the land to raise its elevation. With higher ground, sewers were installed and the town was drained.

Additional clay from the lake was used to make bricks in the Pullman brickyards south of the town. In the winter, many of the brickyard employees then harvested ice from Lake Calumet. (The winter of 1884 resulted in about twenty-five thousand tons of ice stored in icehouses on the shore of the lake.)[110]

WEST OF LAKE CALUMET, 1886

On this map:

- The area to the right of the heavy dark vertical line is in Hyde Park Township.
- The slightly darker area to the left of this line is in Calumet Township.
- The north–south road just east of that township boundary is Michigan Avenue.
- Residential areas in each township appear gray but have fine diagonal lines.
- The heavy, slightly diagonal line that extends the length of the map left of Pullman is the Illinois Central Railroad.
- Roseland straddles the northern part of that township line. In later years, Roseland expanded eastward to the Illinois Central tracks.

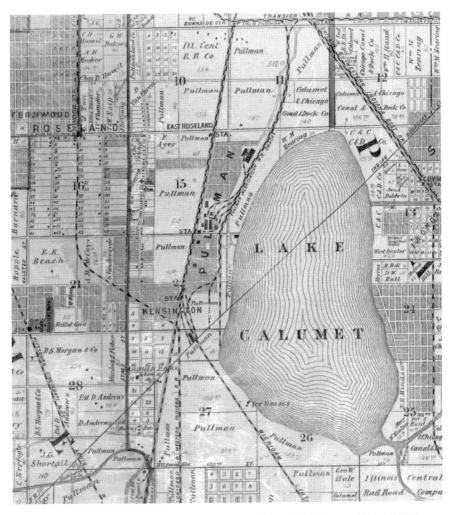

Lake Calumet area from Snyder's Real Estate Map of Cook, Du Page and Part of Will Counties, Illinois. *L.M. Snyder & Co., 1886.*

- Kensington was also west of the Illinois Central tracks but southwest of Pullman.
- Generally, blank areas were either farmland or undeveloped open prairie or wetland.

Note all the lands around the town of Pullman that were owned by Pullman.

DESIGNING A MODEL TOWN

In 1879, George Pullman hired three locally well-known professionals to help him design the perfect working community: landscape architect Nathaniel Barrett to design the layout of the town; civil engineer Benzette Williams to design water and gas lines, sewers and overall drainage; and architect S.S. Beman to design the buildings.[111] The architectural styles and generally red brick that was used in most of the manufacturing, residential, commercial and public buildings give a visual cohesiveness to the town that still exists today. Some bricks were fashioned at Pullman's brick works,[112] then south of today's 115th Street.[113] The finer-looking Indiana Pressed Red Face Brick came from the brickyards in Porter, Indiana.[114]

The "town" of Pullman, a thoroughly planned industrial/commercial/residential complex, was unlike any other American urban venture.[115] Surveying the property began on April 24, 1880.[116] Construction then got underway on May 25 and was nearly completed in just four years, a marvel for its time.[117] A few more blocks were built in 1888 and 1892.

THE PARKLIKE LANDSCAPE

Nathaniel Barrett's parklike design for Pullman was radically different from then-typical blue-collar urban industrial communities. This town would have tree-lined streets, open green spaces and front and back yards for all the housing units. Residential areas would be separate from the shops. By 1885, there were 30,000 trees bordering the streets,[118] and company employees did all the landscape maintenance.[119] The Pullman company had a greenhouse and nursery located at the east end of 112th Street (then next to Lake Calumet) that provided more than 100,000 flowering plants to the community each year.

LAKE VISTA. In his attempt to combine beauty with efficiency, Nathaniel Barrett designed a lagoon, Lake Vista, for the front of the Administration Clock Tower Building. The lagoon would collect condensation from the giant Corliss engine that powered the Pullman Car Works while also serving as a reflecting pool for the distinctive building.

One hundred years later, in the book *Pullman: Portrait of a Landmark Community*, Nancy Miller reprinted a description of this scene written by an eighty-eight-year-old woman who was just six years old when she and her mother arrived in town:

I came to Pullman from Scotland in May, 1891. My father had come here three years before us to work for Pullman. We got off the train at the depot, and there was Lake Vista. There were lovely trees on each side of the street and everybody had grass and lawns. You could see from the train that they had PULLMAN spelled out by Lake Vista, and I knew we were here. [See the front cover and illustration on page 63.]

—*Anonymous*[120]

PULLMAN AVENUE (now Cottage Grove) in its original form was a winding carriage road that extended south from 108th Street, passing in front of the Allen Paper Car Wheel Works, meandering between the Administration Clock Tower Building and Lake Vista and ending at the front door of the Arcade Building on 112th Street. It was straightened and moved to its present location in about 1900 when Lake Vista was filled in shortly after George Pullman's death.[121]

INTERSECTION CIRCLE FLOWERBEDS. Nathaniel Barrett softened the town's rather formal grid system with several circular flowerbeds at street intersections. One of them, pictured here in 1890, was at the intersection

The southwest view from the Clock Tower, circa 1890, Lake Vista on the far right. S.S. Beman also designed the two churches on the horizon. They were built outside of town but still on Pullman-owned land. *By Wylie Denson, Pullman National Monument Preservation Society.*

of Pullman Avenue and Florence Boulevard (now 111th Street and Cottage Grove Avenue). Years later, as most of the residents had their own automobiles, the flowerbeds were deemed an impediment to traffic and removed.

STREETS AND YARDS. Nathaniel Barrett's design included broad streets with wide cobblestone gutters. All the streets and alleys were macadamized (the pavement material at that time). The front yards extended sixteen to twenty-five feet from the public way, making the housing units closer to the street than in many other neighborhoods. In order to adequately maintain the town's trees, flowers and lawns, he set aside six acres on the lakeshore, between 112th and 114th Streets, for a nursery and greenhouse.[122]

STREET NAMES. Many of the north–south streets were named after well-known inventors: from west to east were Pullman, Morse, Watt, Stephenson, Fulton, Whitney, Cottage Grove, Erickson (originally probably Ericsson) and Bessemer Avenues. The numbered streets followed the Chicago street numbering system except 111th Street, which was originally Florence Boulevard, named after George Pullman's eldest daughter. After the sale of the nonindustrial buildings in 1907–9, the street names and addresses were changed to match the Chicago system.

ARCADE PARK, due east of the Arcade Building and immediately south of Hotel Florence, had a formal garden. Its center contained a display with

Arcade Park, mid-1890s. Market Hall is the tall building on the left. *Courtesy of Pullman State Historic Site.*

thousands of bright annuals all arranged in specific geometric patterns. Surrounding it were dozens of native plants and shrubs resembling a more natural area.[123] It was here that, beginning in 1886,[124] the Pullman band gave its series of summer concerts.

PULLMAN PARK was the other public open space area within the town that was part of the town's entrance area. West of the Hotel Florence, it was simply a pastoral green space interspersed with a few trees. Both parks are now maintained by the Chicago Park District and Pullman community volunteers.[125]

WATERWORKS AND DRAINAGE

Many, if not most, communities on earth are older than their utilities. But not so with Pullman. It was Benzette Williams's job to plan for these utilities before the community was built, and he created a system that was ahead of its time. Although Lake Calumet was right next to his community, it was too shallow and its vegetation would have quickly clogged any intake pipes, so

Left to right: The machine shop, water tower and Corliss engine shop. *Beberdick*.

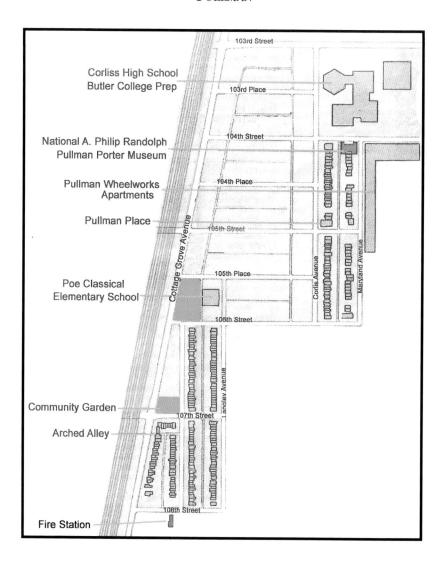

like the city of Chicago, Pullman had to either use well water (which it did at first) or get its water from Lake Michigan, which it then did.

The water was pumped to town in thirty-inch main lines to the huge Pullman water tower, and from there it was dispersed throughout the town. The water tower was destroyed in 1957 when the plant's main smokestack was being demolished and accidently set the tower on fire.

Nearly a century ahead of its time, Pullman had separate stormwater and sanitary sewers. The stormwater ended up in Lake Calumet while the sewage water was drained into a large tank under the water tower and then

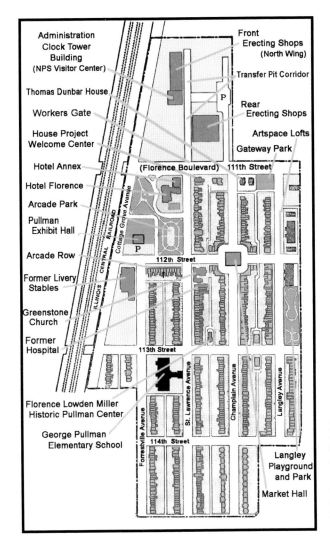

Opposite: The north Pullman neighborhood as it is today. *HPF/KJ Schoon.*

Left: The industrial area and the south Pullman neighborhood as they are today. *HPF/KJ Schoon.*

pumped to a 170-acre farm two miles south of town, where it was used as fertilizer.[126]

It's been claimed that in 1896 Pullman's sewage system was a factor in Prague's International Hygienic and Pharmaceutical Exposition naming Pullman the "world's most perfect town."[127] Because it was used as a fertilizer, unlike today, even Pullman's sewage was considered an asset not to be wasted.

THE BUILDINGS

With the Great Chicago Fire still a vivid memory, Pullman was designed to be a nearly all-brick town with pitched and mansard roofs made of natural slate.[128] To a large extent, architect S.S. Beman designed the buildings in somewhat of an innovative Queen Anne style. The town's visual continuity identified it as a well-planned, integrated community in which industrial and residential buildings complemented each other.

The industrial buildings occupied the center of the development, with residential buildings to the north and south. Most of the public buildings were in the southern section of the town—south of 111th Street (formerly Florence Boulevard).

Once construction began in 1880, it proceeded at a furious pace. More than one hundred railroad carloads of supplies arrived weekly. Industrial buildings were started first—after all there was no need for residences for workers if there was no place to work. The first tenant moved into his Pullman home on January 1, 1881. The erecting (woodworking)[129] shops were in business by March of that year, and by spring, six hundred residents were living in Pullman homes.[130]

Nathan Barrett and S.S. Beman along the decorative wall of the Pullman "front yard," circa 1890. *Courtesy of Pullman State Historic Site.*

THE INDUSTRIAL BUILDINGS

Unlike many other industrial complexes in Chicago and other cities, the Pullman Works buildings north of the broad Florence Boulevard (now 111th Street) were designed to be architecturally pleasing in a parklike setting. The red brick exterior walls reflected the appearance of much of the public and residential housing, particularly the closest housing units that were located on the south side of Florence Boulevard.

Each industrial building had its own purpose in the assembly process. And because Pullman was a planned community, each individual industrial building was placed in such a way as to save time and motion as railcars were being built. As Pullman did not want to waste anything, the wood shavings and even the sawdust from the erecting shops were collected and used to augment the fuel for the huge Corliss engine[131] that provided the energy to run the plant.

Until the twentieth century, most visitors arrived in Pullman on the Illinois Central Railroad. Therefore, as they arrived, the first buildings they saw were

Pullman's attractive "front yard," circa 1893. If you look carefully, you can see PULLMAN on the lawn to the left of the clock tower. *Courtesy of Pullman State Historic Site.*

The Allen Paper Car Wheel Company plant also faced the Illinois Central Railroad. Allen's executive home can be seen on the far left. *By Thomas S. Johnson, Courtesy of Pullman State Historic Site.*

the depot and the impressive Administration Clock Tower Building. For this reason, Architect S.S. Beman had the clock tower face the tracks rather than the town. In front of these buildings was Lake Vista with its fountain and an ornamental stone wall. The clock tower and flanking erecting shops on either side created an impressive "front yard" for the town.

According to Robert W. Bartsch, who worked at Pullman from 1906 to 1956, the clock in the clock tower was run by large weights, which, as they slowly descended, powered the clock mechanism. It took two men, once a week, to rewind the clock. He said that two of the clock's faces showed Standard Time and two showed "railroad time."[132]

The building north of and similar in design to the Pullman clock tower and shops housed the Allen Paper Car Wheel Company. That firm, which made compressed "paper wheels" for railroad cars, and a nearby residence were leased to the company's founder and owner Richard Allen. The Pullman Palace Car Company was, not surprisingly, its largest customer.

The building complex was demolished in 1957 as part of an urban renewal program.

"Paper car wheels" is a misnomer—they were iron or steel wheels with a mass of compressed paper inside. The earliest railroad cars had cast-iron wheels, which were sturdy but unfortunately allowed all the bumps and unevenness of the tracks to be delivered to the car's passengers. This resulted in a noisy and bumpy ride.

It was Richard Allen of Vermont, a former locomotive engineer, who invented wheels with paper cores. The paper, however, was compressed so tightly that it was as hard as ivory, but "spongy" enough that it absorbed much of the bumpiness of traveling on the rails and thus softened the ride.

The Allen Paper Car Wheel Company started making these wheels in 1868 but had few if any customers until 1870, when George Pullman bought a set. Mr. Pullman was so pleased with the smooth ride that they gave his passenger cars that he started using them for all his passenger cars. In 1881, Allen built his main plant in the town of Pullman. As the company sold more wheels to Pullman than to any other line, it made sense for it to build its largest shop near its biggest customer. Mr. Allen then moved to Pullman to be the superintendent of the plant.[133]

After about ten years, the company orders fell. The new problem was that the change from wood to steel cars made the cars heavier and with trains then going faster than before, there was more stress on the wheels. At the same time new steel technology made the wheels obsolete.

The Union Foundry made cast-iron wheels, among other things, for freight cars. It had two large buildings about a quarter mile north of, and closer to the lake than, the Pullman car works.

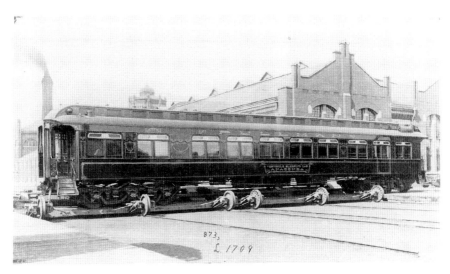

The Pullman sleeping car, circa 1889. *Petraitis collection.*

THE PUBLIC BUILDINGS

The PULLMAN DEPOT was built next to the Illinois Central tracks where they are crossed by 111th Street (then Florence Boulevard). It was through this station that most workers and clients arrived. When the tracks were elevated in the 1920s, the depot was moved west of the tracks, and eventually the building was torn down in order to build a parking lot.

As the clock tower served as the front yard to the town, the HOTEL FLORENCE and other public buildings did the same for the south residential area. Hotel Florence, named for George Pullman's oldest child and one of the two most elaborate buildings in town, was the first nonindustrial building constructed. Built to impress, the adjacent park originally had no trees that might hide the hotel from view. The four-story hotel with its 16-foot-wide, 268-foot wrap-around veranda[134] opened in November 1881 with sixty-five guest rooms.[135]

The hotel's exterior was made of red brick with a steep slate roof. The top floor contained a "fanciful roof of gables and dormer windows."[136] Even the chimneys were elaborately designed with rich detail.[137]

The Pullman depot on the Illinois Central line. *Courtesy of Pullman State Historic Site.*

Postcard of the four-story Hotel Florence. *Photo by H.R. Koopman; Petraitis collection.*

Pullman waiters and the Hotel Florence dining room, 1882. *Photo by H.R. Koopman, Petraitis collection.*

Several rooms had large, open fireplaces.[138] The building was equipped with gas lighting; heat was provided through radiators by steam, which was generated by the Corliss engine on the plant grounds on the north side of Florence Boulevard (now 111th Street).[139] The elegant large dining room, with a capacity of more than one hundred guests, served exquisite meals. President Ulysses S. Grant dined there when he visited the town.[140] The kitchen extension is not original. It is said that it was hastily added when the new German chef complained to George Pullman that the hotel's kitchen area was simply too small.[141] The chef and other staff had rooms above the kitchen.

The first floor had a ladies' parlor, but the rest of the floor, consisting of a reading room, barbershop, billiard room, bar and office, was similar to a private club for gentlemen. The wood trim was made of polished cherry. As with other similar establishments in the Victorian age, unaccompanied women were not permitted to register.

The second floor had a private suite of rooms reserved for the Pullman family (which they seldom used, as their Prairie Avenue home wasn't that far away). The other rooms on that floor were the largest, most lavish and most expensive guest rooms in the hotel. Guest rooms on the third and fourth floors were smaller and, naturally, cost less per night. The rooms were furnished with armoires for the guests' clothing. None had closets. Only the suites at the end of each hallway on the second and third floors had private washrooms. Other guests (as was common at the time) used public washrooms located on each floor. There were, however, separate private bathrooms that guests could use if they made arrangements with the hotel's maid.

The hotel and its bar were not intended for Pullman workers; its prices were generally beyond their means. The *Chicago Evening Post* noted that it was at the Hotel Florence where "the aristocracy of Pullman hold forth."[142] The hotel made a profit its first year. The adjacent hotel annex was built in 1914.[143]

The massive and elaborate ARCADE, the largest nonindustrial building in town, was completed in 1883. It and the Market Hall were the two retail buildings in Pullman. Nearly a century before indoor malls became common throughout the country, all shopping there could be done conveniently while protected from wind, rain and snow. The Arcade occupied the entire city block between 111th Place and 112th Street, from Pullman (now Cottage Grove) Avenue to Morse (now Forrestville) Avenue.

The Arcade Building southwest of the Hotel Florence, the largest Pullman building in the south Pullman neighborhood. *Courtesy of Pullman State Historic Site.*

The two-story Arcade Court bathed in natural sunlight. The sign near the back reads, "To the people of Pullman, Roseland and Kensington, Save time and carfare by buying your goods at Arcade Mercantile Co. at Lowest Chicago Prices." *Courtesy of Pullman State Historic Site.*

The Arcade was covered by a slate roof, but the court had a roof of glass that allowed sunlight to stream in. The building also housed a post office, the Pullman Loan and Savings Bank, the library, town offices, rentable storefront spaces for private businesses and a theater with seats upholstered in dark red leather.[144] The theater could be rented to outside groups, but the management attempted to host only moral presentations and amusements.[145] There were offices for doctors, dentists and others. The third floor had lodge rooms. The YMCA and Methodist, Baptist and Episcopalian churches rented space in there as well.[146]

The 1883 business directory of Pullman listed a barbershop, tailor, dressmaker, billiard hall, drugstore and restaurant in addition to stores selling shoes, cigars, clothes, groceries and dry goods, hardware, hats, sewing machines and stoves—all within the Arcade.

The Arcade's theater, the "Pride of Pullman"[147] was said to be the finest theater west of the Hudson River—that is, until the Auditorium Theatre was built in downtown Chicago. The theater was beautifully ornamented, and patrons entered from a grand staircase in the lobby. The prices of admission at thirty-five, fifty and seventy-five cents were less expensive than the Chicago theaters.[148] The most expensive seats were in the balcony's boxes close to the stage. All presentations had to meet George Pullman's moral standards. He and his family attended several shows each year.

Performances ranged from professional programs also playing downtown Chicago to community theater groups composed of interested residents. The theater turned out to be too large for a community the size of Pullman. A good-sized audience might still leave half the seats empty. In 1902, five years after the death of George Pullman, the theater's greatest patron, the theater closed "for lack of patronage."

The five-room Pullman library and its six thousand books were the gift of Harriett and George Pullman. Library memberships cost three dollars a year for adults (seventy dollars in today's money) and one dollar a year for persons under the age of eighteen (twenty-four dollars today).* Yet with twelve thousand residents in town, the library membership never was larger than two hundred persons.[149] All funds collected went toward purchasing more books. The Pullman Palace Car Company paid all the expenses of running the library. After 1908, library services were free.

The library was housed on the second floor in four elegant rooms with stained-glass windows, chandeliers and upholstered furniture, which gave them the aura of a gentlemen's club. The fifth room was a plain reading

---

* Free "public" libraries were still a rarity as late the 1880s.

The Arcade Theatre, a somewhat distorted view created by reversing the original photo on the right and placing it to the left of the original. *Courtesy of Pullman State Historic Site.*

room with a separate entrance for Pullman workers who might not feel comfortable in the other rooms. Residents could attend art, language or literature classes or learn stenography in the evenings. The librarian was Bertha Ludlam, George Pullman's cousin.

As nearby shopping areas in Roseland and Kensington took away customers in the 1920s, the Arcade Building lost retail renters and soon became a liability. It was demolished in 1927. In 1953, an American Legion hall was built on this site. The Historic Pullman Foundation later purchased that building and in 1993 made it the Historic Pullman Visitor Center.

MARKET HALL was built on a square right in the middle of the intersection of 112th Street and Stephenson (now Champlain) Avenue. The ground level contained sixteen stalls that were leased to private food vendors. Folks came here to buy meats, fruits and vegetables. Apparently for sanitary reasons, the Pullman administration didn't want groceries in the Arcade. The upper level had offices and a meeting hall. Probably the most famous speaker in

The main reading room in the Arcade's library. *Petraitis collection.*

The original Market Hall, built in 1881. *Courtesy of Pullman State Historic Site.*

the hall's large meeting room was Clarence Darrow, who in 1891 gave a speech titled "The Eight-Hour Workday and How to Obtain It,"[150] a talk that George Pullman might not have allowed if he knew of the topic ahead of the event.

Market Hall may have the saddest history in that it burned three times. The original Market Hall building, built in 1881, was destroyed by fire on April 7, 1892,[151] one year before the opening of Chicago's World's Fair of 1893. George Pullman didn't want World's Fair visitors to see it in ruins, so he had it rebuilt in six months.

In 1893, the new structure, similar to the original, but with Romanesque arches, also had rented market stalls where folks could purchase fresh foods and meeting/multipurpose rooms above. The upper floors were occasionally used for dances and exhibitions.[152]

The second fire in 1931 resulted in the upper two floors being destroyed, and they were removed, leaving a one-story building. During the Depression, there just wasn't enough money to rebuild them. The third fire was in 1973.

The GREENSTONE CHURCH AND PARSONAGE is faced with a rare greenish metamorphic rock called serpentine stone, which was quarried in Pennsylvania. The building was dedicated in 1882 by George Pullman's younger brother, the Universalist Reverend James M. Pullman.[153]

The new Market Hall, built in 1893. The Market Square apartments are visible on both sides. *Courtesy of Pullman State Historic Site.*

The Broadhead Meat Market, circa 1895. *Courtesy of Pullman State Historic Site.*

According to an early member, "Mr. Pullman [who was also a Universalist] anticipated that the building would house a community church to which all the residents would belong. That didn't happen. In 1881, the heads of fifteen families were brought together to organize the church. A plan was laid out, and there was optimistic assent until the question of what cleric was to lead the church was considered. Each denominational group would participate only with a minister from its tradition. Each group then went its own direction."[154]

Naturally, the residents of Pullman wished to worship as they had before moving to the town, and as a result of its high rent, the Greenstone Church sat empty for three years.[155] During that time, the various religious groups began renting rooms in the Arcade, the Casino or Market Hall. Undoubtedly, some of the smaller groups met in members' houses. Although George Pullman was a religious man, he noted that the church structure was built "[in this prominent location] for the completion of the artistic effect of the scene."[156]

Finally, in 1885, the required rent was lowered by two-thirds, and a Presbyterian congregation used the building until 1907. Then after several requests by Roman Catholics and by Swedish Lutherans, George Pullman

The Greenstone Church and parsonage from Arcade Park, showing all four corners of the intersection of 112th Street and St. Lawrence Avenue, circa 1890. *Petraitis collection.*

agreed to lease land to them west of town (and therefore not within the historic district) on 113th Street so that they, using his architect S.S. Beman, could build their own church buildings.

These two church buildings can be seen faintly on the horizon of the photograph on page 57. In 1907, when the Pullman Company had to sell its nonindustrial holdings, the Greenstone Church was purchased by the Methodist Church, which still uses it. The building's interior is not much changed. The congregation still uses the original Steere and Turner organ, built in 1882, one of the few manual tracker organs still operating in the country.

The FIRE STATION with its nine-story[157] watch and hose-drying tower was designed by Solon Beman and built in the north residential area on 108th Street in 1894. It was first operated by the Pullman company to serve north Pullman and the industrial area. The City of Chicago now owns the building, which is now the last firehouse in Chicago with a such a tower. By 1956, the city had vacated the building, but in 2012 it authorized necessary tuck-pointing, masonry stabilization and roof repairs.

MASONIC HALL on 113th Street was originally built as a boardinghouse for single men. In 1907, as the Pullman Company was selling its nonindustrial buildings, it was purchased by Pullman Chapter No. 204, Royal Arch Masons,[158] which converted the second and third floors into a lodge room with a balcony. It is now known as the Florence Lowden Miller Historic Pullman Center and is the headquarters of the Historic Pullman Foundation.

The LIVERY STABLES on 112th Street were for horses owned by guests and wealthier employees. The town had no barns, even for residents who owned their own horses and buggies.[159] Folks who needed a horse or carriage could rent one here. For a while, the building also had a barbershop and a telegraph office.

The building housed the Pullman fire brigade and its water wagon for a time. The firemen slept upstairs and did use a fireman's pole to quickly get down to the first floor. Fire hydrants, using pressure from the Pullman water tower, were installed throughout the town.[160]

Immediately south of the Greenstone Church on St. Lawrence (formerly Watt) Avenue, the PULLMAN HOSPITAL was originally a boardinghouse. In 1907, it was purchased by Dr. Floyd Moore, who formed the Pullman Hospital Association in 1908[161] and converted the building into a small hospital. It served that purpose until the Roseland Hospital was opened in

Opposite, top: The Greenstone Church sanctuary, circa 1906. *Photo by H.R. Koopman; Petraitis collection.*

Opposite, bottom: Masonic Hall, 1955. Today the Florence Lowden Miller Historic Pullman Center. *Petraitis collection.*

Above: The fire department entrance to the stables, circa 1885. *Petraitis collection.*

Above: A postcard showing the hospital and adjacent residential buildings, circa 1915. The porch was not original and has since been replaced by one historically appropriate. *Courtesy of Pullman State Historic Site.*

Opposite, top: The Casino. *Courtesy of Pullman State Historic Site.*

Opposite, bottom: The original Pullman Elementary School building. *Courtesy of Pullman State Historic Site.*

1925. When it was returned to its original use, a home for residents, the elevator shaft was converted into bathrooms on each floor.

The CASINO,* between the livery stables and the original Pullman Elementary School, was unusual in that it looked quite different from other Pullman buildings. The first floor held the town's maintenance department office, the town photographer and the town undertaker. At various time, the second floor was used by both Episcopal and Methodist Episcopal congregations. The building was demolished in the 1920s and replaced with a laundry.

PULLMAN ELEMENTARY SCHOOL was originally located north of 113th Street and south of the Casino on Cottage Grove (formerly Pullman) Avenue.

---

* In nineteenth-century America, the name referred not to a gambling enterprise but to a social club or a public building where civic functions or enjoyable activities took place.

The second and current Pullman Elementary School building. *Courtesy of Pullman State Historic Site.*

George Pullman was in favor of education, so the school was free to all Pullman residents. The building proved to be too small, and two wings were added to the building.

It was parents of children at this school who petitioned the Illinois Central to build an elevated track, not so much that traffic could pass unhindered underneath, but to make it safer for the children and other pedestrians. Even with the additions, the school proved to be too small to accommodate all the students in town. In 1910, Pullman Elementary School was replaced with the current school building on Forrestville Avenue. The "new" building, designed by Dwight Perkins, is one of only a few Chicago schools listed in the National Register of Historic Places.

What Pullman did not have was TAVERNS. However, this lack was countered by all those in Kensington,[162] nearby, but outside Pullman town borders.

11

PULLMAN

Residences and Early Residents

S.S. Beman designed the residence buildings so that the first floor and front entrance were about seven steps higher than ground level. This made the basements partially above ground and allowed for windows and ventilation; it also kept the basement floor above the water table so that it wouldn't flood. Folks in town were of course pleased that all the residential units in town had basements that were "dry enough to reside or sleep in."[163]

All Pullman residential buildings contained indoor plumbing[164] as well as indoor gas for lighting and cooking,[165] and most units were more spacious than workers could afford in other parts of the Chicago area.[166] Every residential unit had both a small front and back yard. Alleys behind the houses were used by vendors as well as for trash removal, done daily by Pullman employees.[167] Pullman housing was a company investment, and rents, as well as charges for heat, gas and water were adjusted so that the company could receive its hoped-for 6 percent return on its considerable investment in housing stock.

As originally built and except for the units at the ends of row housing, the row house units were just two rooms deep so that windows could provide each room with natural sunlight and ventilation. An extra window, seldom seen in houses today, is the transom over the back door. In the days before air conditioning, transoms helped cool a house by providing a way for warm air near the ceiling to flow out of the building—particularly important to row houses because (except for the units at the ends) they didn't have side windows. Skylights provided additional lighting for the top floors.[168]

Residents on the front porch of a house on Morse (now Forrestville) Avenue. *Courtesy of Pullman State Historic Site.*

There was no requirement for employees to live in the town. Originally, units were rented only to employees of the Pullman company, but that changed over time. But no residences were for sale. All were owned by the Pullman Land Association.

The housing units were of varying sizes. To save space and lower heating costs, all (or nearly all) were row houses; the larger, more elegant residences, were just duplexes (which allowed for additional windows). Residents rented what they could afford. Unskilled laborers and foremen usually lived in the smallest units and paid the lowest rent. Skilled laborers could afford larger units and managers and executives the largest—with the highest rents. Single men were often housed in boardinghouses or tenement blocks with shared kitchens.[169]

New employees with no children would likely choose to live in one of the smaller units. Then as their families increased in size, or as they were promoted and earned bigger salaries, they might very well choose to move

Dinner in a Pullman flat. Unknown artist. *Petraitis collection.*

to a larger home. The workers didn't have to worry about forgetting to pay their rent on time, as rent was originally deducted from their paychecks. When that practice became illegal, the company issued two checks every payday: The amount on one equaled what was owed in rent; the other had the balance. The paymaster then had the employees endorse the "rent" check over to the company.

The homes were heated with steam or coal-burning stoves. All units, except some in the tenements, had water and gas piped in. The average rent for small apartments, flats and single-family row homes was fourteen dollars per month.

After visiting Pullman in 1884, Johns Hopkins University professor Richard Ely described the residential area as having a "unity of design and an unexpected variety," which charmed him as he wandered through the town. "Simple but ingenious designs secure variety: French roofs, square roofs, dormer windows, turrets, sharp points, blunt points, triangles, irregular quadrangles, are devices resorted to in the upper stories to avoid the appearance of unbroken uniformity....No other feature of Pullman can receive praise needing so little qualification as its architecture."[170]

COTTAGES. Each cottage row house was a single-family home with its own front door. They were two stories tall plus a basement. Most had five rooms: a living room and kitchen with a pantry on the first floor and three bedrooms plus a lavatory on the second. There were small closets on both floors. These five-room units rented for seventeen dollars a month. Larger units with seven rooms had a bathroom, fireplace, formal dining room and four bedrooms and, of course, cost more to rent.

TENEMENTS. On the east side of Fulton (now Langley) Avenue between 111th and 113th Streets were large apartment buildings, identified by the letters A through F, where up to five hundred persons, many of them newly arrived immigrants, lived. Although there was indoor plumbing, there was but one common water faucet for every five families.[171]

TWO-FLAT ROW HOUSES. Mixed in all the blocks with the average cottage row houses were two-flat row houses. These buildings were wider and

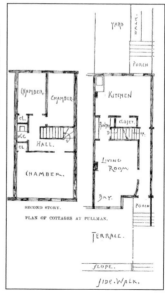

Above: Cottage row houses on the west side of the 11200 block of Langley Avenue, 1973. This is a great example of how S.S. Beman created different front façades to relieve the monotony of row housing. These units had two skylights: one over the stairway and one over the bathroom. *By Paul Petraitis.*

Right: A cottage floor plan. These units were sixteen feet wide. *Public domain.*

Looking north at three-flat apartment housing built in 1882 on the 11300 block of Fulton (now Langley) Avenue, circa 1885. The front doors originally led to three separate apartments, each with four rooms (living room, eat-in kitchen and two bedrooms and water closet (wc/toilet and sink). *Petraitis collection.*

had a separate apartment on each floor. Each unit had four or five rooms, consisting of a living room, kitchen, lavatory and two or three bedrooms. There was storage in the basement.

THREE-FLAT ROW HOUSES had front doors that originally led to three separate apartments, each with four rooms (living room, eat-in kitchen and two bedrooms and water closet [toilet and sink]).

HONEYMOON ROW on the 11400 block of Champlain (formerly Stephenson) Avenue. Each side consisted of twelve units with four or five small apartments each with a "living" room (also used for cooking and eating), a pantry with a sink and two small bedrooms but no bathroom nor kitchen. The common hallway on the first floor had four lavatories each with a toilet and sink. Though called "honeymoon row" because of the small size and low rent, these apartments were often used not only by young families starting out but also larger families who couldn't afford anything more expensive.

APARTMENT buildings such as those on Fulton (now Langley) Avenue had front doors that originally led to three separate apartments, each with four rooms (living room, eat-in kitchen and two bedrooms and water closet). Today, some residents have converted their apartments by merging them into more spacious single-family homes.

MARKET HALL APARTMENTS grace the four corners of Market Hall Square in which Market Hall once stood. Built in 1893, they were designed to reflect the architecture of the new Market Hall. They have curved colonnaded fronts with Florentine arches and have three apartments (with bathrooms) each, one on the first floor and two on the second floor. As they were finished

Above: Market Hall Apartments. Watercolor by Sylvia DeYoung. *Used with permission; Sylvia DeYoung.*

Opposite, top: Arcade Row houses on 112th Street. *Courtesy of Pullman State Historic Site.*

Opposite, bottom: Elegant duplexes on Executive Row, the southeast corner of 111th and Champlain, circa 1883. A maid looking out the front door can be seen at the unit on the far right. *Petraitis collection.*

at the time of the World's Fair, George Pullman used these new buildings to house special visitors from the fair.

FOREMAN'S ROW AND SKILLED CRAFTSMAN ROW. The 11100 and 11200 block of St. Lawrence (formerly Watt) Avenue consisted of single-family row house units with six or seven rooms, many featured dining rooms and full bathrooms.

ARCADE ROW. The spacious and elegantly designed three-story units on 112th Street tended to house executives, managers and teachers. These homes featured a parlor, formal dining room, kitchen, fireplaces, full bath and six or more bedrooms. In the 1890s, Chicago mayor John Hopkins,[172] who had been a Pullman employee, lived on Arcade Row.

EXECUTIVE ROW units were duplexes on Florence Boulevard (now 111th Street) facing the Pullman car works. They were Pullman's largest, most beautiful and most expensive homes. They had formal dining rooms, double

parlors, several fireplaces and the most spacious yards. Being the closest homes to the plant meant that the executives had the shortest walk to work and didn't have to go through the blue-collar neighborhoods to get there or to the Hotel Florence, the Arcade, the Greenstone Church or the livery stables. Some of the occupants had live-in maids.

NORTH PULLMAN residences were built around the same time as those in south Pullman, but the Pullman company ceased construction in 1885. Being distant from the public buildings south of the plant, these units were harder to rent. Besides housing Pullman employees, the area also had employees of the Union Foundry and the Allen Paper Car Wheel Works. These two companies tended to hire unskilled workers who were paid

Children playing along Erickson (now Maryland) Avenue in north Pullman. *Photo by H.R. Koopman; Petraitis collection.*

less than Pullman employees. So in 1888, the Pullman company began to subdivide some north Pullman homes into flats, with one apartment on each floor. Thus, much of the housing there was less expensive than housing south of the plant.

It should be noted that George Pullman never lived in "his" town; for the rest of his life, he maintained his residence in his opulent mansion on Chicago's south Prairie Avenue. If for some reason he had to stay overnight, or if he wanted some quiet time for himself, he could use his personal suite of rooms at the Hotel Florence.

GEORGE PULLMAN, THE GRAND MARKETER

George Pullman mastered the art of advertising and marketing early on. Then as soon as his plant in the new "town" of Pullman was up and running, his advertising expanded in earnest. The company had spent a lot of money on this venture, and he had to ensure that he would build and lease enough cars to justify the expense. Much of his advertising was at company expense, but free publicity that he encouraged came by way of two primary sources: first the newspaper articles and rave reviews about his sleeping cars and his town, and second, marketing paid for by the rail lines that leased his cars extolling the comfort and service on *their* Pullman cars.

As magazines became popular and their circulation expanded, George Pullman bought full-page ads—and when color was available, he had full-color ads. His ads appeared often in the popular *Saturday Evening Post*. In addition, he took executives and the press on complimentary runs. He exhibited his cars at several world's fairs. For the fairs, he built an impressive and beautiful scale model of the town. And when the World's Columbian Exposition was in Chicago in 1893, he brought tourists to his town to see it for themselves.

THE POPULATION AND COMMUNITY ACTIVITIES

By 1890, the population of Pullman exceeded ten thousand persons.[173] With many immigrant employees from various parts of Europe, the town of Pullman for decades remained ethnically diverse but still racially homogeneous.[174] All (or nearly all) residents were white, and more than half were immigrants from Scandinavia, Germany, Britain, Holland and Ireland.[175]

About 44 percent of Pullman's employees were its African American porters. Since they worked on the trains, not in the Pullman shops, they tended to live in all parts of the country but near, often walking distance to, railroad company hubs that utilized Pullman sleeping cars.

At first, with the standard ten- or eleven-hour workday, workers didn't have a lot of free time. But as there was no television, radio or motion pictures to watch, the Pullman company organized and encouraged its employees and their families to participate in several town-wide activities, including band,

Pullman employees at an erecting shop. *Photo by T.S. Johnson. Courtesy of Pullman State Historic Site.*

Employees at the Pullman Company machine shop, 1920. *Hammond Public Library*.

Employees heading out for lunch. *Petraitis collection*.

Top, left: The "Pullman Boys" baseball team. *Beberdick.*

Top, right: The Pullman cricket team, 1902. For a while, the team practiced on the empty lots that are now Gateway Park. *Courtesy of Pullman State Historic Site.*

Bottom: The grandstand and boathouse on Pullman's Athletic Island. *Courtesy of Pullman State Historic Site.*

orchestra, choral groups, gymnastics, football, cricket and softball, bicycle races and a whist (card game) club.[176]

A ten-acre sports and play area designed by the landscape architect Nathan Barrett was created on "Athletic Island" (actually a peninsula rather than an island) just off the Lake Calumet shoreline. (See the 1889 map on page 15.) The earliest acreage reclaimed from the lake through landfill,[177] it had a running track, a ball field, a grandstand and boathouses. Regattas were held every spring and fall.

Many of Pullman's various sports teams became quite well known. The cricket team was said to have won the "Championship of the West," and the baseball team was called the best "outside of the professional nines."[178] After that facility was no longer available, Pullman residents would find plenty to do at Palmer Park, a later Chicago facility, just west of the Illinois Central tracks and across the street from Pullman Tech.

The Pullman band in front of the north entrance of the Hotel Florence. *Courtesy of Pullman State Historic Site.*

Pullman had a great marching band, one that was good enough in 1893 to be invited to Washington to play for the inauguration of President Grover Cleveland. It was composed of first-class musicians partly because George Pullman offered jobs to good musicians who would come and work for him. The band was said to be, next to Sousa's and the U.S. Marine Band, the best in the nation. It frequently gave free open-air concerts at Arcade Park.[179]

ACCOLADES AND THE WORLD'S FAIR OF 1893

In 1893, Marguerite Doty reflected on George Pullman's plans for the town:

> *Pullman has put the working man upon a higher plane and placed about him conditions which are better than he could have hoped for if unaided....*

*The improved homes and the healthful and convenient shops of
Pullman were created in advance of any expressed demand by workmen
for them*[selves]*....But when they are given such improved homes and
surroundings they are able not only to do better for themselves and their
families, but better in every way for their employers.*[180]

Although some visitors, including social worker Jane Addams,[181] described
the town as a product of George Pullman's philanthropy, Mr. Pullman
himself emphasized that the town was an investment that was built to
provide a profit to the corporation.[182]

George Pullman was so proud of his accomplishments that when
he learned that Chicago was going to host the 1893 World's Columbian
Exposition and it would be held in Jackson Park, just a short distance north
of Pullman, he agreed to be on its executive committee.[183] He also signed on
to have a good-sized exhibit in its Transportation Building.

At the fair, after seeing his exhibit, George Pullman encouraged fairgoers
to make the fifteen-minute trip and see the town of Pullman for themselves.
He had had double-decker streetcars built specially to carry visitors from the

A Pullman lounge car
on display at the 1893
Chicago World's Fair.
*Courtesy of Pullman State
Historic Site.*

The double-decker streetcars. *Courtesy of Pullman State Historic Site.*

fair grounds to the town.[184] Once at the town, they could eat or stay at the hotel, shop at the Arcade, admire the clean new residences, and appreciate the flowers and greenery. Streetcars also ran through the town. Special guests were invited to stay at the brand-new Market Hall Apartments.

The town of Pullman became one of Chicago's premier tourist attractions. In Pullman, garbage was picked up daily and sewage pumped away underground, the streets were lined with healthy trees and every lawn was mowed. And of course, after their time at the fair, visitors from out of town could go back to their hometowns in Pullman cars.[185]

ALMOST EVERYTHING A FAMILY might want was available in Pullman—or so went the official story. It was a nice neighborhood with parks and tree-lined streets, homes for workers larger than what they could afford in Chicago, indoor plumbing (but not necessarily private bathrooms) and walkable stores and businesses. Garbage was picked up daily. The town had nearly everything except a tavern. (But, as noted earlier, nearby Kensington had plenty of them.) However, it differed from most other towns in that it did not have a policy-making town council with members elected by its residents.

Undoubtedly, the first employees and their families were probably happy to move into new Pullman housing. Indoor toilets, running water, spaciousness, proximity to work and retail stores would have at first seemed wonderful. Unfortunately, the general happiness did not last.

12

UNREST, ANNEXATION AND STRIKE

Economics professor Richard Ely visited the still-new town in 1884 and published his evaluation in the February 1885 issue of *Harper's New Monthly Magazine*. Although he acknowledged that the buildings and streets were pleasant, he noted concern about the way George Pullman and his company controlled so much in town. He wrote that a common complaint was that the workers did not feel like the town was really a home; they felt like they were living in a giant hotel. Ely believed that the American desire of home ownership was most commendable. Home ownership gave people a stake in their community. Renting an apartment, townhome or duplex from the Pullman Palace Car Company didn't do that. Ely concluded that the idea of Pullman "is not the American ideal." Rather it "is benevolent, well wishing feudalism, which desires the happiness of the people, but in such way as shall [also] please the authorities."[186]

Several Pullman employees, who could afford to do so, did purchase homes across the tracks in the nearby Roseland community. In fact, the Pullman Savings and Loan Bank, which George Pullman founded in 1883, offered mortgages for some who did.

As early as 1884 (just three years after the Pullman plant opened), 150 employees in the freight car department went on strike when their wages were cut; the company responded by replacing the strikers with workers from Chicago. In 1886, Pullman workers walked off the job in support of a national effort by the Knights of Labor to get an eight-hour day and a 10 percent wage increase. Ten days later, with police protection, the company welcomed the strikers back—but under their old terms.[187]

George Pullman refused to negotiate with his employees. He later told the U.S. Strike Commission that "it would have been unethical for him to give charity [to his employees] at the stockholders' expense." His principal responsibility as president of the company, he went on to say, "was to enhance *their* investment"[188] (emphasis added). A disgruntled employee could always just quit his job and look for employment elsewhere.[189]

In 1888, the *Chicago Tribune* wrote of Pullman:

> *None of the "superior," or "scientific" advantages of the model city will compensate for the restrictions on the freedom of the workmen, the denial of opportunities of ownership, the heedless and vexatious parade of authority, and the sense of injustice arising from the well-founded belief that the charges of the company for rent, heat, gas, water, etc. are excessive—if not extortionate....Pullman may appear all glitter and glow, all gladness and glory to the casual visitor, but there is the deep, dark background of discontent which it would be idle to deny.*[190]

ANNEXATION

The Pullman residential neighborhoods had earlier been classified by Hyde Park Township as "farmland," so the property tax was low. George Pullman justified continuing this classification by noting that his company hardly

used any of the township services and therefore shouldn't have to pay for them.[191] Mr. Pullman liked being outside of Chicago's city limits and away from its control. However, on June 29, 1889, a township-wide referendum was held to determine whether Chicago should be invited to annex the township.

George Pullman strenuously objected to annexation, as his company already provided many of the services (such as water, sewers and road maintenance) that Chicago did. He made the Arcade theater available for anti-annexation rallies and stated that annexation would undo all that had been built up in town. It would mean that "ignorant and corrupt politicians, rather

George Pullman about 1890. *Courtesy of Pullman State Historic Site.*

than competent businessmen" would run the town, and his work toward "order and moral upgrading would disintegrate."[192]

When the votes were counted, the pro-annexation voters township-wide had 62 percent of the vote even though 76 percent of Pullman residents did vote against it.[193] After the referendum, all of Hyde Park Township (including Pullman) was annexed by Chicago. The city then vastly grew in geographic area. Back in 1870, the city contained just 35 square miles; after annexation, it consisted of 185 square miles and had a million residents.[194]

The town of Pullman then became Chicago's thirty-fourth ward. But being part of Chicago didn't alter much at Pullman, as the Pullman Land Association still owned all the land and buildings. And similar to what is done today in many gated communities, the streets continued to be owned by the developer (the Pullman company). The company, not the city, continued to maintain them.

STRIKE

The year 1893 was momentous. Eager for the tax income that railroads provided, midwestern states had licensed far too many rail lines, and in 1893 the country's economic bubble burst. What followed and lasted for four years was the century's most severe economic depression.[195] Fortunately for Chicago," the World's Fair softened its effects for a while.

Orders for rail cars declined, and the Pullman company struggled to pay its stockholders their expected dividends. In an extremely unpopular move, the company decreased workers' salaries but not their rents. And because rents in effect were deducted from workers' paychecks, employees simply had less money for food, clothing and heat. Hundreds of workers took in boarders to augment their income.[196] However, the company did not cut the salaries of its executives, nor did it reduce the dividends paid to stockholders.[197]

To combat general discontent and grievances across the country, a new national organization, the American Railway Union (ARU), was formed for railroad employees. Beginning in March 1894, Pullman workers began joining.[198] Pullman employees were allowed to join the ARU because the company did own a small railroad company that ran into the car works grounds—so in a sense, Pullman employees could be considered railroad employees. The ARU fostered mediation over strikes, and after several successful negotiations, its membership grew to more than 150,000 persons nationwide.[199]

Strikers at Turner Hall, Kensington, circa 1894. Unknown artist. *Petraitis collection.*

Unfortunately for Pullman workers, George Pullman was resolute; his policies dictated company practice, and the Pullman employees' grievance committee was not successful in its negotiations. He personally did meet with the grievance committee on May 9, 1894, not to negotiate, but to inform them that by lowering wages, he was able to keep his employees working.[200] The day after the committee met, three committee members were laid off, officially for reasons unrelated to being on the grievance committee.[201] Nevertheless, the committee called for a strike beginning on May 11. The company still refused to negotiate. Its financial condition was kept afloat because the railroad companies continued to pay Pullman for the use of their sleeping cars.

To support the striking workers, community members formed the Pullman Relief Committee, which collected and distributed food, money and clothing.[202] During the strike, John Hopkins, the mayor of Chicago who had earlier worked for Pullman and who still lived in the town, supported the union. He was invited to speak at a fundraising activity at the Market Hall and raised $1,500 for the strikers.[203] For many families, the aid simply wasn't enough, and they left the Pullman company to find jobs elsewhere.[204]

George Pullman, however, spent most of this time out of town on family and business matters. When he left for New York on June 30, he did not ride in their private car, which might have been recognized by strikers. Instead, he made the trip in a special car on a regular Pennsylvania Railroad train.[205]

The union had insisted that order would be maintained during the strike. It even posted guards to ensure that there was no damage to company buildings. For seven weeks, the town of Pullman was strangely silent. There was even less drinking at nearby taverns.[206]

Pullman's clergy were divided on the issue. The pastor at Pullman's Greenstone Church supported the company, while Reverend William Carwardine, pastor of local Methodist Episcopal Church, which rented space in the Casino, strongly supported the workers. He wrote, "I believe that the town itself was established in the hope of bettering the condition of the laboring classes, but it has failed sadly of is original purpose."[207]

While the strike was going on, in June 1894, Congress passed and President Cleveland signed a resolution making Labor Day a national holiday.[208] Twenty-three states and several cities had previously approved the holiday at a local level.[209]

Stymied by the lack of negotiations, the Pullman workers asked the American Railway Union for assistance.[210] Pullman workers weren't the only ones whose wages had been cut, and as a result, there was a great deal of sympathy for them across the country. And so, when the call for an ARU boycott went out, workers generally supported their Chicago "brothers," which resulted in a widespread boycott of trains carrying Pullman cars. The rail industry, particularly in the Midwest and West, was hit hard. Newspapers across the country carried front-page stories about the effects of the boycott. On July 1, the *New York Times* called the boycott the "Greatest Strike in History."[211] In spite of its early success, the ARU and its president, Eugene Debs, were unhappy that some of his members, or perhaps outsiders, were

National Guard troops at the Hotel Florence. *Courtesy of Pullman State Historic Site.*

sabotaging and vandalizing rail cars. They were fearful that others would use the tense situation as an excuse to start a riot.[212]

Responding to the boycott, the General Managers' Association (GMA), an organization composed of administrators of twenty-four railroad companies, unanimously decided to support the Pullman company.[213] It recommended breaking the boycott, not only by hiring non-union men to replace those refusing to work on trains that carried Pullman cars but also by having its member railroad companies include U.S. mail cars on trains that were carrying Pullman cars. This, they hoped, would force the federal government to issue an injunction against strikers.[214]

When that did occur, it was the first U.S. court injunction used against strikers. Real news, but also rumors, "fake news" and even fake interviews with Eugene Dubs were printed in newspapers across the country. Crowds, described by some as "angry mobs," gathered at rail yards. Numerous states called out their national guards to keep order, and President Cleveland dispatched the military to protect the railroads.[215] But the presence of men in uniform provoked more disorder. Violence broke out at many railyards and continued for several days. Shots were fired at numerous locations, killing a total of thirty persons.

None of these incidents occurred within the town of Pullman, but several were nearby. On July 5, agitators, said to be outsiders, attacked the Chicago Stockyards and that night set fire to forty-eight Illinois Central cars.[216] On the sixth, some seven hundred cars in South Chicago were burned—although

Members of the Illinois National Guard securing the Arcade Building during the 1894 strike. *Courtesy of Pullman State Historic Site.*

there were no Pullman cars there. A U.S. deputy marshal fired into the crowd in Kensington,[217] killing an innocent bystander.[218] The next day, a crowd clashed with the militia in South Chicago, resulting in four rioters being killed and nearly two dozen wounded.[219]

The state militia arrived in Pullman and remained until after the strike ended. Because the ARU decided not to call off its boycott, its leaders were jailed and morale was broken. By July 12, trains were moving again;[220] the boycott and strike faltered and failed.

13

REPERCUSSIONS

The country was divided over where to place blame. Some blasted the unions while others blamed George Pullman and his apparent lack of concern for the welfare of his employees. But George Pullman still felt that his obligations were to his stockholders and board of directors. He was said to have believed that outsiders, who wanted to introduce gambling dens and brothels into Pullman, were responsible for the strike and nearby riots.[221]

Although the company stated that it had no objection to unions, all Pullman employees who walked out and were rehired were required to turn over their union membership cards and sign a statement promising not to join any union while employed by Pullman. Workers not rehired were blacklisted and had trouble finding jobs elsewhere. During the strike, no residents were evicted.

Although the boycott affected about two-thirds of the country, it was widely known as the "Pullman" strike.[222] It was determined afterward that the money that the Pullman company lost during the strike was greater than what it would have cost to give the workers what they had been requesting.[223] Although unsuccessful, the strike/boycott did demonstrate the potential power of national labor unions. After the strike, Illinois governor John Peter Altgeld attempted to persuade George Pullman to help care for his employees who had gone two months without a paycheck but was unsuccessful.

George M. Pullman, circa 1895.
Courtesy of Pullman State Historic Site.

Shortly after the strike ended, President Grover Cleveland established the United States Strike Commission, to which George Pullman provided a detailed explanation of how the plant and town operated. After months of research and hearings, the commission issued a 681-page report largely supporting the workers' efforts. It noted that "the Pullman company is hostile to the idea of conferring with organized labor in the settlement of differences arising between it and its employees."[224] It found that through wage cuts, the company was shifting the hardship of the recession onto its employees with no detriment to its shareholders. The commission asked the rhetorical question, "Why should capital and labor...persist in cutting each other's' throats as a settlement of differences?" Many of its recommendations became part of the National Railway Labor Act thirty-two years later.

DEATH AND LEGACY

George Pullman's life after the strike wasn't much different than before, except that he tired faster than he used to and was becoming more impatient. He had been warned by doctors that his heart was not in good condition. The warning didn't cause him to change his habits, but in July 1897, he did pick out a family burial plot at Chicago's Graceland Cemetery.[225]

George Pullman worked in his downtown office until 5:00 p.m. on October 18, 1897, and before dawn the next morning, he suffered a massive and fatal heart attack. His funeral, held in the Pullman mansion on Prairie Avenue, was attended by his family, close friends and company and city officials.[226] He was then buried in the plot he had selected at Graceland. His casket was covered with tons of concrete, which made grave robbery impossible but also served as a foundation for a tall Corinthian column that can be seen from quite a distance. The simple but noticeable memorial was, at Hattie Pullman's request, designed by the town's architect, S.S. Beman.[227]

At the time of his death, George Pullman's Palace Car Works was the largest railroad car plant on earth, and his company had 90 percent of the North American sleeping car business.[228]

As did many successful Chicago businessmen, George Pullman gave considerable monies to charities, but he did so without pomp and publicity and therefore was not known as a philanthropist. Rather, he is largely known as an inventor, which doesn't really describe him. He did not invent sleeping cars, but he certainly improved them.

He was, however, a great salesman, selling his product to railroad executives and to the traveling public. His brother Albert, who for years supervised the building of the famous Pullman sleeping cars, was more the inventor, or at least the designer.

When he was starting out in New York and Chicago, George Pullman worked alongside his employees. As his successes grew and his company expanded, he removed himself from those who actually were making his cars. He always felt more of an obligation to his board of directors and to the people who risked their monies by investing in his company than to his employees, who knew very little about his constraints and business practices in general.

By the time he died, Pullman was a household name. When travelers said that they had slept on a Pullman, folks knew what was meant. In 1884, Three Forks, Washington, was renamed Pullman, Washington, in honor of George Pullman.

In his will, George Pullman left $1,200,000 to build a school for students living in or working at Pullman.[229] Called the Pullman School of Manual Training, it was situated on land west of the Illinois Central tracks because there was no room for it within the original town.

The Pullman School of Manual Training when it was new in 1915. *Glessner House Museum.*

THE PULLMAN SCHOOL OF MANUAL TRAINING

The Pullman School of Manual Training, often known as Pullman Tech, was built on a beautiful forty-acre campus, just a short walk from the IC tracks. (See map on page 15.) George Pullman's will paid for the school's construction and ongoing management expenses, specifying that tuition would be free for students (who either worked or lived in the town of Pullman).

The school opened its doors in 1915. After running for thirty-five years—and with not enough money to continue its free education—the school closed in 1950, after which an endowment was given to the new George M. Pullman Educational Foundation.

The building reopened the next year as Mendel Catholic High School, a preparatory school for boys. In 1998, it became the Southside College Preparatory Academy and was renamed in 2001 in honor of former U.S. Poet Laureate and South Side resident Gwendolyn Brooks.

The school is now a selective enrollment magnet middle and high school. It was at this facility in 2015 that President Barack Obama declared Pullman to be a National Monument.

14

PULLMAN PORTERS ORGANIZE

T hrough the nineteenth century, race and gender played a big part in what jobs a man or woman could expect to hold. At Pullman, employees from the top executive level down to most unskilled laborers were white men. Most of the skilled laborers were rather young men. But if white and male, one could expect that with experience and hard work, one might get a promotion to a more responsible and higher-paying job. Women were hired as the company needed maids or workers to sew or do laundry. A few women had positions in the shops.[230]

African Americans, both men and women, were hired in service positions. Some became cooks and maids, but by far most were men, and most of them became porters. A porter's job was to carry passengers' luggage, shine their shoes, prepare sleeping berths or private rooms and serve passengers' needs as requested. Conductors, who were in charge of the operations on the Pullman cars, were white.

Next to the maids, porters' salaries were the lowest in the company, and the workdays were the longest—sometimes twenty hours long, with four hours of sleep before the next day of service. And, whereas nearly all of the white employees worked with and lived near other white employees, the Black porters might live in any of the states through which Pullman cars passed. And much of the time they worked alone, serving the needs of the passengers of the cars to which they were assigned.

Even though the porters comprised 44 percent of Pullman Company employees,[231] they were not permitted to join the railroad worker unions,

An 1894 Pullman advertisement. *Library of Congress.*

which were and intended to remain all white. The fear that Black men would take jobs away from white people because they would work for lower wages began soon after the Civil War. This fear affected policies that lasted for generations. Even the constitution of the Order of Sleeping Car Conductors, which represented Pullman's conductors, explicitly excluded African Americans from membership.[232] At the dawn of the twentieth century, forty-three national unions had no Black members.[233] Many racial barriers remained in force until after the Second World War.

Asa Philip Randolph. *Library of Congress.*

In the earliest years of the twentieth century, porters attempted to form their own union, but the Pullman Company quickly fired employees who were known to be union organizers. In an attempt to pacify its porters, the Pullman Company instituted the "Employee Representation Plan," which may have looked like a union but was controlled by the company.[234] Consequently, in 1925, when a union was finally formed, it was organized by the Porters Athletic Association at a meeting of five hundred members in New York, not Chicago.

To prevent the company from firing union members, the organizing group kept its membership secret and then asked Asa Philip Randolph, the editor of the Harlem monthly the *Messenger*, to be its president. After being encouraged to do so by his wife, Lucille, he agreed. The union selected the name the Brotherhood of Sleeping Car Porters and Maids.

Because the new union didn't have much money, A. Philip Randolph served the organization for eleven years before it was able to offer him a regular salary. Fortunately, Lucille owned and operated a successful beauty salon in Harlem and supported both themselves and the Brotherhood. Philip Randolph was a powerful public speaker, but as he was not, nor ever had been, a Pullman employee, he couldn't be fired by the company.

Understandably, the Brotherhood was disliked by the Pullman Company administration. Surprisingly, the organization didn't even have full support of the Black community, as the fear of recriminations was quite real: the Pullman Company might stop hiring African Americans if it wanted to punish the union, or it might stop advertising in Black-owned newspapers.[235] In addition, the union was not supported or even recognized by many of the largely white labor unions already in existence.

Although at first the National Mediation Board (NMB) denied the organization's appeals for help, the Brotherhood did become the first labor organization led by African Americans to receive a charter by the American Federation of Labor (AFL) although at first it was only a second-class "federal" charter that recognized some Brotherhood locals, but not the organization itself.[236]

African American women played a large part in sustaining the Brotherhood. Because many of its activities needed to be kept secret from the company, members' wives and sisters organized meetings, collected dues and encouraged nonmember porters to join.[237] These women, many of whom were not Pullman employees, formed their own sections of the Brotherhood: Women's Economic Councils and the Ladies Auxiliary to the Brotherhood of Sleeping Car Porters. These were the nation's first labor organizations created by African American women. Pullman maids, though actual company employees, were often advised to join the auxiliary or one of the councils.[238] As there were far fewer sleeping car maids than porters, the membership of the Brotherhood was primarily male and its focus tended to be largely on improving the lot of the porters. At that time, it was believed by many that an improvement in working men's status would benefit women as well. Eventually, "Maids" was dropped from the organization's name.[239]

The Brotherhood grew but then had great difficulty surviving during the early years of the Great Depression. Membership dwindled, and its office phone and electric service were cut off because it didn't have enough money to pay its bills. When Congress amended the Railway Labor Act in

A Brotherhood, mass meeting Chicago, 1933. *Chicago History Museum.*

1934 and made "company unions" such as the Employee Representation Plan illegal, the Pullman Company simply replaced it with the "Pullman Porters Protective Association," formed by porters who were supported by the company.

It had taken ten difficult years for Randolph to organize the Pullman porters, who were working on several different railroad lines, into a cohesive group. But by 1935, he finally had an organization strong enough that it could claim to represent all the porters, even though fewer than half were actual members.[240] The NMB then organized an election in which the porters and maids chose the Brotherhood over the company's Protective Association as its preferred exclusive collective bargaining agent.[241]

The Brotherhood was certified by the NMB that same year. Formal negotiations with the Pullman Company began, and two years later, in 1937, the Brotherhood and the company signed their first collective bargaining agreement. That contract resulted in a raise in salaries, better security and the creation of an agreed-upon means by which employees could submit grievances. This action was the first contract ever agreed to by a major U.S. corporation and an African American union.[242]

AFTER THE CONTRACT

Recognizing the national significance of the Brotherhood's 1937 contract, that year the NAACP's magazine, *Crisis*, noted, "As important as is this lucrative contract as a labor victory to the Pullman porters, it is even more important to the Negro race as a whole, from the point of view of the Negro's uphill climb for respect, recognition and influence, and economic advance."[243] The success of the Brotherhood and the resultant improvement in salaries helped establish the Black middle class. Porters then were earning enough money that they could purchase property and pay poll taxes that allowed them to vote. And being protected by their union, they didn't fear arbitrary dismissal, as many other Black workers at the time did.[244]

In 1941, as American defense industries were building up steam, A. Philip Randolph proposed a massive march on Washington to bring attention to widespread employment discrimination that prevented African Americans from sharing in the post-Depression economic opportunities that were expanding, particularly in the defense industries. The goal of the march was to bring pressure on Congress and the president to establish policies making discrimination on the basis of "race, color, religion or national origin" illegal.[245] He canceled the march when, a week before it was to take place, President Roosevelt agreed to issue an executive order desegregating war industries and prohibiting hiring discrimination in programs connected with federal contracts. Eventually respected by both Black and white union members outside the Brotherhood, A. Philip Randolph, in 1955, helped negotiate the merger of the CIO and the AFL and then served as an AFL-CIO vice president.

Also in 1955, former Pullman porter and Brotherhood member E.D. Nixon was one of the organizers of the Montgomery, Alabama bus boycott. He was the one who encouraged the young Reverend Martin Luther King Jr. to lead the boycott[246] that then propelled Dr. King into a leadership position in the civil rights movement.

In 1963, Randolph not surprisingly was named chairman of the March on Washington. While Dr. King's speech is the one best remembered from that event, Philip Randolph also spoke from the podium that day:

> *Let the nation know the meaning of our numbers. We are not a pressure group. We are not an organization. We are not a mob. We are the advance guard of a massive moral revolution that is not confined to the Negro, nor is it confined to civil rights, for our white allies know that they are not free while we are not.*

In 1964, President Lyndon Johnson awarded A. Philip Randolph the Presidential Medal of Freedom. The National A. Philip Randolph Pullman

A. Philip Randolph, congratulated by President Lyndon Johnson as he received the Presidential Medal of Freedom. *Lyndon Johnson Library.*

The A. Philip Randolph Pullman Porter Museum in the north Pullman neighborhood. *Schoon.*

Porter Museum, established in 1995,[247] is located in the north Pullman neighborhood at 10406 South Maryland Avenue. The museum is a three-story facility with displays on all three floors. Tours generally begin with a documentary about the Brotherhood.

15

THE PULLMAN COMPANY
AND THE TOWN 1897–1945

After George Pullman's death in 1897, Robert Todd Lincoln, the Pullman general counsel and the son of the sixteenth U.S. president, was named acting president of the Pullman Palace Car Company. Four years later, his title was changed to president.[248]

As president, Robert Lincoln changed the form of company administration from the one-man proprietorship led in the past by George Pullman to a more modern bureaucratic management system. He also oversaw the change of Pullman sleeping cars from wood to all-steel construction; from gas lighting to 32-volt direct current electricity; and from the exceedingly-ornate Victorian interiors to a simple elegance of clear wood and Mission-style molding.[249] Then in 1899, he managed the takeover of the Wagner Car Company, the Pullman Company's last major competitor. At this point, all sleeping cars were being made by the Pullman Company.[250]

In 1898, the Illinois Supreme Court ruled that the Pullman Company had exceeded its rights and ordered it to sell all nonindustrial properties. After a ten-year period to prepare the land and buildings for sale, between July 1907 and February 1909, all residences and public buildings were sold. The company did give residents first option on their own homes.[251] As the company sold its residential and commercial properties, it discontinued maintaining the buildings, streets and parks, and the physical appearance of the town declined.[252] Robert Lincoln served as president of the company until his retirement in 1911 and then served as chairman of the board of directors for another eleven years.

Right: Robert Todd Lincoln, Pullman's second president. *Library of Congress.*

Below: Erecting Shop B, the second of three large shops built on "made land" when parts of Lake Calumet were filled in. Courtesy of Pullman State Historic Site.

By this time, the town of Pullman was getting cramped, as it had filled all the building spaces between the Illinois Central railroad tracks and Lake Calumet. One option that remained was expanding eastward by filling in western parts of the lake. So new industrial buildings were built on acres of "made land."

The building of Athletic Island, Pullman's first move eastward into the lake, was done in the early 1880s by dumping tons of clay from (likely) basement excavations in the town. In 1898, the year that the Illinois Supreme Court ordered the Pullman Company to sell all nonindustrial properties, the company found that the grandstand timbers were rotting and decided to raze the athletic structures, create more land around it and build a needed round house, the last building that S.S. Beman designed for the town.

RACIAL SEGREGATION ON THE TRAIN

Many Jim Crow laws in the South, which mandated racial segregation, were in effect from the end of Reconstruction in 1877 to 1965. They were upheld by the U.S. Supreme Court in 1896, which then required "separate but equal" accommodations for African Americans.

While not outlawing segregation, the Interstate Commerce Act of 1941 still allowed rail lines to require that white and Black passengers ride in separate cars, but the rail lines could not discriminate in the accommodations that were present in the different sections. In addition, carriers could not offer poorer accommodations to African Americans who were paying the same fare as white passengers, but they could offer those services in a segregated area.

As Pullman cars were used in the South, those cars were required to abide by Jim Crow regulations. Conductors were charged with telling passengers

A segregated passenger car. Note the "Colored" sign on the partition next to the passageway. *Courtesy of Pullman State Historic Site.*

where they should sit, and Black passengers who refused to sit in "colored" sections could be ejected from the train. The Pullman Company was allowed to have separate cars for white and Black passengers or could use partitions to separate the races. Conductors were given "police powers" to enforce segregated seating.[253] Many of these practices continued until 1964, when the Civil Rights Act ended legal segregation.

EXPANSION: THE EARLY TWENTIETH CENTURY

On January 1, 1900, having completed its acquisitions of competing companies while diversifying its product line, the Pullman Palace Car Company was reorganized and took the name Pullman Company. By then, the City of Chicago had annexed Hyde Park Township and started altering the landscape and the streets. Lake Vista was drained and filled in, and Cottage Grove Avenue was straightened and made parallel with the Illinois Central tracks. The tracks then were elevated to allow traffic to pass underneath, and the train station was moved to the west side of the tracks.[254]

After 1909, when residential housing units were all sold, the street names were gradually changed to Chicago names. Cottage Grove (in north Pullman) was changed to Corliss (after the inventor of the Corliss engine), Erickson became Maryland, Pullman became Cottage Grove, Morse became Forrestville, Watt became St. Lawrence, Stephenson was changed to Champlain, Fulton became Langley and Florence Boulevard was changed to 111th Street.

Pullman Cars in the East

A Lehigh Valley 1900 timetable, under the heading "Handsomest Train in the World," boasted that its coaches were observation cars built by Pullman.
It noted that its train had:

• comfortable smoking rooms,
• both a ladies' and a gentlemen's lavatory,
• polished Mexican mahogany panels,
• ceilings of the new Empire dome pattern, finished in white and gold, and
• beveled French plate mirrors.

The last car on that train, with seating for just twenty-eight passengers, was a magnificent Pullman Palace Car, with plate-glass windows and wicker chairs.

Pullman Cars in the West

In March 1907, Pullman built a steel sleeping car named the *Jamestown*, which was exhibited at the Jamestown Exhibition in Virginia. To build steel cars, the south erecting shop at 111th Street and Cottage Grove Avenue had to be enlarged. But to do this, the pleasing symmetrical design of the Clock Tower Administration Building and its shops on either side disappeared.

As the company made this switch to all-steel car production, many of the skilled carpenters were no longer needed. A large number of them then moved away and were replaced by unskilled newly arrived immigrants largely from southern and eastern Europe.[255] By 1910, Pullman was building five hundred steel cars a year. These heavy cars were said to be the most comfortable railroad cars ever built, before or since.[256]

In 1910, the Pullman Company began the construction of its freight car shops on 103rd Street. In later years, this plant produced wing sections for U.S. Army transport airplanes.

All this time, the Pullman Company continued its advertising campaigns, often running full-page ads in popular magazines. The ad pictured on the following page from the *Atlantic Monthly* was particularly noteworthy, as it described why Pullman cars were not just comfortable but safe and healthy. The trains' sturdiness and sanitary conditions were pointed out,

Passengers in a Pullman parlor car on the Oriental Limited enjoy the trip while a Pullman porter vacuums the floor, circa 1910. *Petraitis collection.*

Above: A steel car under construction, 1915. *Courtesy of Pullman State Historic Site.*

Left: An advertisement in the *Atlantic Monthly*, 1916, emphasizing safety from both injuries and illness: The trains' sturdiness and sanitary conditions are pointed out, in a justification for moving away from Victorian opulence and toward the simpler, smoother, "Mission" stylings. *Courtesy of Pullman State Historic Site.*

Pullman stewards in the galley. *Petraitis collection.*

and in a justification for moving away from Victorian opulence and toward the simpler, smoother, "Mission" stylings, one ad emphasized, "Smooth painted surfaces, sanitary floors, the avoidance of heavy hangings, scientific ventilation, and adequate screening eliminates…the dust and dirt of railway travel. Systematic cleaning and frequent chemical fumigation are used to create 'a constant state of cleanliness and sanitation.'"

souvenir

MENU

Left: The Sessions Pullman Club Restaurant souvenir menu created for the ninth annual Pullman House Tour, 1982. *Courtesy of Pullman State Historic Site.*

Below: Joseph Guest and his delivery truck in front of his bakery on St. Lawrence Avenue, circa 1916. *Courtesy of Pullman State Historic Site.*

With land and buildings owned by private individuals, the town began to change. Because neither Pullman nor Chicago had any zoning laws until 1923,[257] landowners could do as they wished and could afford.

The house at 605 East 111th Street was one of those properties whose change was most noted. It was the largest of all Pullman residences. Originally, it was the home of Henry H. Sessions, superintendent of manufacturing operations at the Pullman plant.* It had high ceilings, double parlors, seven fireplaces and a room set aside for his staff. After the Sessions family moved out, the building became the home of the Pullman Executive Club. Later it served as a banquet hall, a VFW post and, most famously, as a restaurant known at various times as the Sessions Pullman Club, The Retreat and Mercks. After being vacant for some time, it became the House Project Welcome Center.

---

* Henry Sessions patented the accordion-sided connecting vestibule that allowed passengers and staff to walk from one rail car to another while the train was in motion.

This elegant duplex had a speakeasy in its basement during Prohibition. *Petraitis collection.*

In 1910, Irish immigrant Joseph Guest moved to Pullman and worked as the chef and manager of the Pullman Executive Club. Two years later, he bought a house on the west side of St. Lawrence Avenue and, in 1916, built a bakery and grocery store north of his house in the backyard of the block's corner house. In later years, this building housed Bob's Sugar Bowl and later still the Pullman Café.

The Pullman Company continued to grow into the mid-1920s, which was its most successful decade. By the middle of the decade, Pullman's fleet stood at 9,800 cars served by 12,000 porters. At that time, 100,000 passengers (more than the total of all the guests in all the first-class hotels in the nation) were sleeping nightly in Pullman cars.[258]

In 1922, the company merged with the freight railcar maker Haskell & Barker Co. of Michigan City, Indiana. Edward F. Cary, head of the Michigan City plant, was then named Pullman's president.

One might think that the 1919 adoption of the Eighteenth Amendment to the U.S. Constitution prohibiting alcoholic beverages would not have affected Pullman since it had no taverns. But Pullman was certainly affected, because all the taverns in adjacent Kensington were shut down, and Pullman residents who enjoyed a glass of wine, beer or something harder had their regular supplies cut off. But, according to author Nancy Miller, speakeasies flourished during Prohibition, and alcohol flowed in the streets whenever such places were raided by federal Prohibition agents.

Once the Twenty-First Amendment was adopted on December 5, 1933, repealing the Eighteenth Amendment, taverns reappeared in the area, some, according to Miller, run by former speakeasy operators.[259] After Prohibition,

THE HASKELL & BARKER CAR COMPANY, MICHIGAN CITY

The first rail car manufacturing plant in the Chicago/Calumet Area was established in Michigan City, Indiana, in 1852, the same year that the first rail lines from the east reached Chicago. That was the wagon and freight car firm Sherman, Haskell & Company. Three years later, grain dealer John Barker joined the firm, and the name was changed to Haskell and Barker Car Company (H&B). Besides freight and passenger cars, at first the firm produced a wide variety of agricultural vehicles, including reapers, threshing machines and corn shellers. It also produced passenger cars, but only until about 1860, at which time it was finishing two freight cars every day.

By 1910, the Michigan City company employed 3,500 men and was producing 10,000 cars a year. In 1916, H&B was purchased by a group headed by Edward F. Cary. In 1920, the plant, said to be then the largest freight car builder in the country, had 34 buildings spread out over 116 acres in the northwest part of the city.[260]

In 1922, H&B was acquired by the Pullman Company, and Cary assumed the Pullman presidency. In 1934, the plant in Michigan City was renamed Haskell & Barker Shops of Pullman-Standard. During the Second World War, the Michigan City plant produced more than 2,400 sleeping cars for the U.S. armed forces (the first passenger cars made there since 1860). In 1957, Charlton Harper, author of **Railway Car Builders of the United States & Canada** *claimed that the Pullman-Standard plant in Michigan City was the largest freight car plant in the entire world.*[261]

With a significant drop in orders for cars, Pullman-Standard permanently closed the plant in 1971. Many of the plant's buildings were consumed by fire two years later. Lighthouse Place Premium Outlet Mall opened at that site in 1987.

Michigan City's Haskell-Barker plant, 1916. *Petraitis collection.*

The bar at the Hotel Florence. *Courtesy of Pullman State Historic Site.*

the bar that had been in the Hotel Florence's annex was moved into what had been the original billiards room.

By 1925, the Pullman fleet stood at 9,800 rail cars. Throughout these years, the company also made automobile bodies for Packard and other automobile companies.[262] After this time, and as a direct result of the growing popularity of the automobile, orders for new rail cars dropped off and the company began to shrink.

PULLMAN BRANCH OF THE CHICAGO PUBLIC LIBRARY

In 1927, the year that Pullman's massive Arcade, with its large library, was razed, the board of trustees of the Pullman Free School of Manual Training donated land and Harriett Pullman, George Pullman's widow, donated funds to the City of Chicago in order to build the "Pullman branch" of the Chicago Public Library.[263] The library was built west of the Illinois Central

The Pullman Branch Library in 2020. *Schoon.*

tracks on the grounds of the school, which through his will George Pullman had financed thirty years earlier.

Arthur F. Hussander, who drew the plans for more than sixty Chicago public school buildings, designed the library. As this building was to be next to the school, he chose a classical appearance that reflected the appearance of the school rather than something to match the buildings across the tracks in the historic Pullman neighborhood. Consequently, classical Corinthian pilasters (half columns) grace the exterior.[264]

In 1999, resident Andrea Moore Alton described her early memories of that building:

> *The library was my haven and to this day I measure all libraries against the memory of the quiet elegance of its polished oak moldings and smooth marble steps, the fountain just inside the doors where kids used to flock on hot summer days. The acres of tables with their hard backed chairs, and the hushed silence of the cool, high vaulted ceilings.*[265]

The Calumet Historical Society met in that building for many years. Its members collected and cataloged hundreds of photographs of the Roseland/Pullman area, which they kept at the library. These collections are now in the special collections at the main library downtown.

STANDARD STEEL CAR COMPANY, HAMMOND, INDIANA

The Standard Steel Car Company was founded in Butler, Pennsylvania in 1902 at a time when American railroad companies needed new cars faster than they could be manufactured. Its name reflected the fact that it was one of the first companies to make all-steel rail cars. Even before construction of its plant began, the company had orders for six thousand rail cars. The new plant was half a mile long and said to be the longest building in the world. Except for the wheels on its freight cars, the company manufactured all its own parts.

Desirous of a facility close to the Chicago market, in 1906 the company built an immense plant in the Maywood section of Hammond. Located north of 165th Street a few blocks east of Columbia Avenue (and within eleven miles from Pullman by road), the plant made both wooden and steel freight and passenger railroad cars. The 360-acre plant grew quickly and by 1915 employed 2,500 workers, many of whom were Black or Eastern European immigrants. It soon became the city's largest employer.[266] During World War I, the plant produced heavy artillery for the U.S. Army.[267]

Top: Hammond Standard Car Works, Hammond, Indiana, only eleven miles from Pullman. *Northwest Indiana Genealogical Society.*

Bottom: Shift change at Hammond Works, Standard Steel Car Company. *Hammond Public Library.*

ANOTHER MAJOR ACQUISITION

The Great Depression ended the Pullman Company's years of prosperity. But just two months after the stock market crash in 1929, and before people knew how long and devastating the ensuing depression would last, Pullman purchased controlling interest in the Standard Steel Car Company of neighboring Hammond, Indiana. Five years later, the two companies merged boards and formed the Pullman-Standard Car Manufacturing Company.[268]

Due to the economy and new competition from the growing popularity of the automobile, travel on trains decreased during the Depression (1929–1939). In expanding its freight car capabilities, the Pullman Company was investing in long-term growth.

UNEXPECTED PUBLICITY IN 1933

In 1933, Warner Brothers gave the Pullman-Standard Company publicity that has probably been seen by more people than any one ad that the company ever paid for. That year Warner Brothers came out with the smash-hit movie musical *42nd Street*, which has a famous night-time scene filmed in a set made to look like a Pullman sleeper with double-decker berths along the coach's aisle, each berth covered by a dark curtain, giving the passengers (all chorus girls) a modicum of privacy.

The song "Shuffle off to Buffalo" is sung by a newly married couple, while the chorus girls, in their silky pajamas, poke their heads out from behind the curtains and sing along.

One of the song's lines goes:

> *For a little silver quarter;*
> *We can have the Pullman porter;*
> *Turn the lights down low.*

Then, at the end of this scene, the passengers all return to bed and the porter goes through the coach picking up the ladies' shoes and, with a yawn, begins to shine them. It is interesting that thirty-five years after the death of George Pullman, the name *Pullman porter* was still recognizable as an attendant on railroad sleeping cars.

Right: Una Merkle and Ginger Rogers in a Pullman upper berth from the 1933 film *42ⁿᵈ Street*. *Hometowns to Hollywood.*

Below: Male and female employees of the Aircraft Division, 1945. *Courtesy of Pullman State Historic Site.*

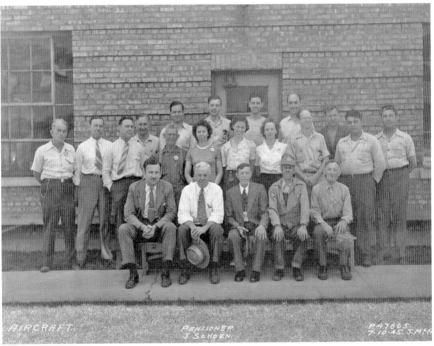

In 1940, the U.S. government filed an antitrust complaint against the Pullman-Standard Company, seeking to separate the company's manufacturing and sleeping car operations. It took four years, but in 1944, the court ordered Pullman-Standard to sell either its manufacturing or operating divisions. The company decided on the latter. With that decision, the company stopped employing porters.

The Observation Lounge is one of the sparkling departures which has gained for this train, the *Southern Belle*, the reputation of "providing all the extras at no extra fare." For its privileges, including radio, magazine racks, and game facilities, are available to all passengers without additional charge.

The Cafe Lounge is spacious. Its tables well separated ... its walls, ceilings and floor completely insulated so that neither crowding nor noise nor hurried service spoil your enjoyment of truly delicious food.

The Skyline Bar decorated in huge murals and luxurious modern appointments provides a cosmopolitan background against which to encounter old friends or enjoy encounters with new acquaintances.

Another Illustrious Streamliner—
SOUTHERN BELLE
OWNED AND OPERATED BY KANSAS CITY SOUTHERN—LOUISIANA & ARKANSAS LINES
BUILT BY PULLMAN-STANDARD
THE WORLD'S LARGEST BUILDERS OF RAILROAD AND TRANSIT EQUIPMENT

The Chair Car, like all other units on this modern train, is completely air-conditioned and, in it, the comfort of passengers is deftly administered by registered stewardess nurses as well as trained *Southern Belle* porters.

In addition to railroad passenger cars, Pullman-Standard designs and manufactures freight, subway, elevated and street cars, trackless trolleys, air-conditioning systems, chilled tread car wheels and a complete line of car repair parts. A large percentage of this company's productive capacity is also engaged in the manufacture of defense material.

In purchasing this magnificent new streamliner, *Southern Belle*, for service between Kansas City and New Orleans, the Kansas City Southern—Louisiana & Arkansas Lines acted on the sound principle that no consideration should outweigh safety ... so they specified Pullman-Standard Construction.

There are no safer trains than Pullman-Standard's

Out of Pullman-Standard's 82 year experience ... out of research before it gave streamlining to America ... out of its constant constructive work with the physical properties of all available fabricating materials ... and out of the privilege it has had for more than twenty-five years of collaborating periodically with the government and the railroads in establishing the specifications for strength and safety to which all railroad equipment should

be built, have come the Pullman-Standard trains whose strength and safety are exceeded by no others now in service.

Your enthusiastic patronage has made streamliners possible and profitable

As a result of their safety, no less than beauty and luxury, Pullman-Standard's streamliners have established the two other most envied records in railroading: 1) the most popular trains in operation; 2) the most profitable trains. But in the last analysis these have been your achievement. You, the public, have made them possible through demonstrating your overwhelming preference for Pullman-Standard streamliners by filling them to capacity as fast as they have gone into service! And the railroads have answered by buying 70%* of the new equipment they have purchased from Pullman-Standard.

PULLMAN-STANDARD CAR MANUFACTURING COMPANY—CHICAGO
Copyright 1941, by Pullman-Standard Car Manufacturing Company   *When this advertisement was written

"*Tops*" IN STREAMLINERS ARE BUILT BY *Pullman-Standard*

A 1941 magazine advertisement. *Courtesy of Pullman State Historic Site.*

Male and female Hammond plant employees doing an inspection. *Courtesy of Pullman State Historic Site.*

Hammond plant employees applying electric brake mechanisms. *Courtesy of Pullman State Historic Site.*

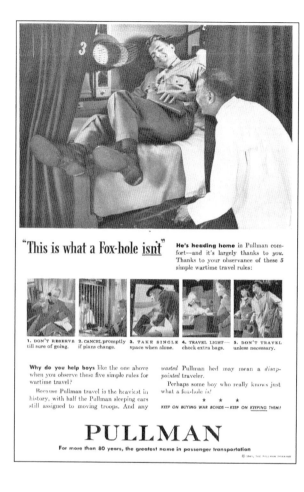

A 1945 ad published before the end of the war encouraging readers to buy and not cash in war bonds and to NOT travel unless necessary. *Courtesy of Pullman State Historic Site.*

In the early 1940s, Roseland resident Adelaide Teninga accepted a position in the manager's office at Pullman-Standard for five dollars a month more than she had been making. She later wrote:

For the next thirty years, I worked in the manager's office, under the Clock Tower, as receptionist, file clerk, Western Union and Postal Telegraph operator, secretary, and later administrative assistant to the Personnel Manager, Harold Sherman. Pullman-Standard was tooling up for World War II. It was a sad day when that stately, wrought-iron fence surrounding Palmer Park was removed to help make war material. Five different unions replaced the old Pullman-Standard Employee Union as many thousands of employees were added to the rolls to build aeroplane wings for Douglas Aircraft and ships for the English and U.S. Navies.

It was during that five-year war period (1940–1945) that many women took on the jobs usually held by men, and lifestyles were permanently changed.

During the war, the Pullman-Standard Chicago plant took full advantage of its location next to Lake Calumet by using a shipyard in the lake to produce thirty-four patrol craft and forty-four medium landing ships. Subassembly of many of the boat sections, though, was done at the shops on 111th Street. The Hammond, Indiana plant was also involved in the war effort, producing artillery for the U.S. Army.

16

THE POSTWAR YEARS

After the war, the Pullman-Standard Company continued to use advertising in print media to entice readers to take a train ride in a Pullman car. However, results were below expectations, as ridership declined again in spite of the country's postwar boom. Yet in 1951, the company made headlines by building the world's first full-length dome car.[269]

Many of Pullman-Standard's advertising campaigns used full-page ads in magazines such as the *Saturday Evening Post* and *National Geographic Magazine*. Two advertising themes that Pullman-Standard employed for many decades were comfort and safety.

Community activities, whether sponsored by the Pullman-Standard Company or private groups continued to provide opportunities for social and sporting events.

After the second fire at Market Hall, in 1931, the upper floors were removed and the lower floors cleaned up, covered with a new roof and rented to private vendors, including a liquor store—an unthinkable tenant during George Pullman's lifetime.

Then on December 16, 1973, a third fire gutted the interior. Again, there was no one with deep pockets to rebuild it. In 1995, the Landmarks Preservation Council of Illinois placed the building on its list of the ten most endangered properties in the state.

In 1958, the Pullman-Standard Company moved its manufacturing operations still located in the historic "town" of Pullman to a location closer to the new I-94 Calumet (now Bishop Ford) Expressway, effectively

Bottom, right: A full-page 1950 magazine ad for traveling by Pullman. *Courtesy of Pullman State Historic Site.*

Bottom, left: A 1946 magazine advertisement promoting its "day-nite" coaches for the Northern Pacific Railroad. *Courtesy of Pullman State Historic Site.*

Top: Even the complimentary bars of soap in the private sleeping rooms promoted the company's reputation for safety. *Schoon.*

shutting down the old plant that had been centered on the Clock Tower for more than seventy years. Many of its old industrial buildings were demolished at this time. Fortunately, those historic buildings facing Cottage Grove Avenue were not taken down.

On January 1, 1969, Pullman-Standard ceased production of its iconic sleeping cars. The next year, the company closed both its main Chicago plant (no longer in the town of Pullman) and its plant in Michigan City.[270] The Hammond plant and some others at remote locations remained open for another twelve years.[271] In 1987, the company sold much of its eastern industrial acreage between 105th and 111th Streets to Ryerson & Son Inc., a subsidiary of the Inland Steel Company.[272] For several more years, the Pullman Company was kept alive, as it made rapid-transit cars and Amtrak's bilevel *Superliners.*

Postscript: Folks who would like to experience riding and sleeping on Pullman-built sleeping cars can still do so. A number of rail-tourist companies offer special overnight trips that include service on actual Pullman dining and sleeping cars.

AMTRAK

Amtrak is a federal railroad passenger service that provides medium and long-distance service between cities in the contiguous United States as well as to nine Canadian cities.

At the beginning of the twentieth century, railroads carried 98 percent of passengers going from city to city. (Riverboats carried the other 2 percent.) The growing popularity of the automobile and later travel by air decimated the rail passenger numbers. By 1957, only 32 percent of intercity travel was by rail.[273]

As passenger service in the United States declined after World War II, its future in the country was in doubt. Rail lines discontinued some routes while offering fewer trips on the routes that they kept active. Those

Pullman-Standard softball team Merchandise Mart League champions, 1952. *Courtesy of Pullman State Historic Site.*

Pullman-Standard softball team Merchandise Mart League awards dinner, 1952. *Courtesy of Pullman State Historic Site.*

Market Hall, as a one-story building. The Market Hall Apartments can be seen in the back, 1955. *Courtesy of Pullman State Historic Site.*

actions, of course, made rail travel even more difficult, and thus they also contributed to the decline.

One by one, the rail lines proposed cutting or discontinuing passenger service. In an attempt to save passenger service, in October 1970, Congress passed, and President Richard Nixon signed, the Rail Passenger Service Act creating "Railpax," which almost immediately changed its name to "Amtrak."

Amtrak saved passenger service in 1971. Soon, Amtrak had to replace many of the old cars that had been running on the various rail lines. Pullman-Standard won the contract for that order, which included specifications for 102 coaches, 70 sleepers, 39 diners, 25 café/lounge cars and 48 coach-baggage cars.[274] Made at the plant in Hammond, the first cars were to delivered to Amtrak in October 1978.[275] Although Pullman-Standard was again making rail cars, including sleepers, the engineers and workers had to follow Amtrak's specifications, not Pullman's.

Amtrak named its new passenger cars *Superliner*. They were air-conditioned and had a stainless-steel exterior design that gave them a sleek, aerodynamic appearance. The bilevel passenger coaches had sixty-two seats on the upper level and fifteen seats and restrooms below. The dining cars' upper levels contained eighteen tables for four passengers each, seating seventy-two passengers, and a central serving area. The lower level had an all-electric kitchen. The sleeping cars had four levels of accommodations, from the small roomettes to the larger family and deluxe bedrooms and an accessible bedroom designed for passengers in wheelchairs.

The Chicago to Seattle *Empire Builder* was the first line to carry these *Superliner* cars; the inaugural trip featured champagne and souvenir buttons. Pullman-Standard's last car in this order was completed on Friday, May 22, 1981, a day that was marked with a catered "last meal" for the employees. The atmosphere in the shop that day was compared to that at a funeral. For when the workmen completed their work on the car, the shop permanently closed. That last car was numbered 32009, and it was noted that the first Pullman car was "Number 9." Consequently, the car was named the *George M. Pullman*, and a brass plaque noting this was affixed to a partition at the top of its stairs.

That year also saw Pullman-Standard become a wholly owned subsidiary of Wheelabrator-Frye Inc. so that it could serve as a holding company in the transportation industry.

PLANNED DEMOLITION OF THE ORIGINAL TOWN

Back in the 1950s, the United States and Canada started construction on the St. Lawrence Seaway. It was then expected that, when the Seaway was completed, a bevy of oceangoing ships would be coming to Chicago. To prepare for this influx, the harbor at Lake Calumet was deepened and enlarged so it could serve international shipping. The harbor improvements were completed in 1956, and plans were made to revitalize the area around the lake.

Then, in 1960, with the original Pullman car works in the town closed, the housing stock about eighty years old and many of its longtime residents gone, the City of Chicago published a new policy recommending clearing and rebuilding "blighted and deteriorating areas" within the city—and Pullman was listed as one of those areas. The local chamber of commerce and a nearby developer then proposed that all the buildings south of 111th Street be razed so that the area could be marketed as an industrial park.

17

CITIZEN INVOLVEMENT AND PRIDE, RESTORATION AND RECOGNITION

M any Pullman residents were shocked that "outsiders" wanted to demolish their neighborhood and planned a meeting at the Greenstone Church to discuss options. Concerned residents filled the building with an overflow out onto the sidewalk. The group decided to reactivate the Pullman Civic Organization (PCO), which had been created during World War II as a civil defense group.[276] Officers were elected, committees formed, articles written for local newspapers and annual picnics held in Arcade Park.

Early plans of this nonprofit organization included a railroad museum in the empty Clock Tower Building.[277] Most importantly, the unique history of Pullman was spread through the community and to city officials. "Old" and, of course, "historic" became positive descriptions. Homeowners not only cleaned up the appearance of their own homes, through the PCO, they banded together to make the whole neighborhood special as well.[278]

The PCO is a co-sponsor of the annual Pullman House Tour; it provides information to new residents and still publishes a monthly newsletter, *The Pullman Flyer*, which keeps residents informed about the greater community happenings.

Another concern arose a few years later when a local developer wanted to tear down some of the original car works buildings and replace them with a budget motel. It then became necessary to convince various government officials that Pullman should be designated a historic district or landmark.[279]

In 1968, the organization applied for and received a grant from the Illinois Arts Council to establish a community archives, which would be

THE PULLMAN FAÇADE LEGACY PROJECT

The Pullman Civic Organization's Beman Committee, named in honor of Pullman's architect S.S. Beman is a volunteer group of architects, preservation professionals and others who have a passion for historic preservation. It has won several awards for its efforts to help residents restore their historic homes. This project has documented what each of the south Pullman houses looked like back when it was built and assists homeowners willing to restore their house's exteriors to that original appearance.

S.S. Beman designed the 616 single- and multi-family homes in South Pullman to be alike enough to make the community look coherent and different enough to provide a pleasing diversity. Of the 616 original units, 613 are still standing. On these 613 units there are 27 styles of doors, 23 window styles and 16 styles of porches, 107 different façade types in all.

To date, its volunteers have compiled architectural drawings that illustrate the original design intention for each historic home in the South Pullman neighborhood. It has also collected old photographs and original Beman drawings of these homes.

Between 2007 and 2012, all of the South Pullman historic homes were inventoried to determine which ones still had their original windows, doors and porches. Surprisingly, only 32 percent retained at least one original window, door or porch. In addition to the Pullman Façade Legacy Project, the Beman Committee has published a Pullman Homeowner Guide and established the Pullman Façade Reimbursement Program whereby residents may apply for a partial reimbursement of up to $1,000, which must be matched at least dollar for dollar by the homeowner. These reimbursement funds are raised by the community fundraising projects and events.

needed in order to obtain landmark designation. This grant spawned the Beman Committee, formed that same year, which still focuses on historic preservation through its Façade Legacy Project.[280]

In 1968, the PCO's organizing and education efforts resulted in the State of Illinois designating the industrial area and the Hotel Florence as a State Historic District. The next year, Pullman's original industrial area and southern residential portion was listed in both the Illinois and the National Register of Historic Places. Then, in 1970, the entire Pullman district from 103rd Street south to 115th Street was designated a National Historic Landmark District.[281]

To further protect the historic integrity, the majority of property owners in south Pullman petitioned to become a city landmark district. Two years later, the Chicago City Council designated the original industrial area and the southern portion of Pullman a "City of Chicago Landmark District." In 1993, the five original residential blocks, firehouse and wheelworks in the northern neighborhood were also made a Chicago landmark district. Then in 1999, the two districts were merged to form the city's Pullman District. City status as a landmark district means that the buildings are protected for current and future generations; owners may either maintain what they have or restore their street-facing façades to their original design.

Realizing that all these efforts would cost money, the Historic Pullman Foundation was established in 1973 to raise funds that could be used to preserve and restore historic Pullman buildings while also supporting research and long-range planning. Since its formation, the foundation has acquired Market Hall; the American Legion building, which became its visitor center; Masonic Hall (which it named the Historic Pullman Center, later revised to Florence Lowden Miller Historic Pullman Center), its headquarters and storage facility; and the Hotel Florence. After purchasing the hotel, the foundation began restoring that building's exterior and its first two floors. It also reopened the hotel's popular restaurant.[282]

Since 1974, the foundation has co-sponsored the annual Pullman House Tour and since 1996 the annual holiday season Pullman Candlelight Tour. It has also organized fundraisers such as clambakes and Christmas Victorian dinners in the hotel dining room. For several years, a group called Friends of the Florence held additional fundraisers.[283] The community has been able to partner with outside organizations as well. One example is the Illinois Labor History Society, which has conducted tours of the town. In 2016, the foundation provided temporary spaces for National Park Service offices in the Florence Lowden Miller Center.

Living in Pullman During Its Centennial Year

In 1980, the Chicago Council on Fine Arts, working with the city's Architect's Office, commissioned photographer Fred Leavitt to photograph the Pullman neighborhood and its people and then publicly display his best shots. The next year, the Historic Pullman Foundation board decided that Leavitt's collection of photographs deserved a wider audience than the exhibition allowed and so published the photos in book form. The following are a few of the photos of Pullman people from that book. They are reprinted here with permission from Mr. Leavitt.

Repainting the porch roof at the Historic Pullman Center. *By Fred Leavitt.*

Left: Preparing the rose garden at the Hotel Florence. *By Fred Leavitt.*

Below: A lemonade stand, many kids' first business venture. *By Fred Leavitt.*

A choir and organ performance at the Greenstone Church. *By Fred Leavitt.*

The ice cream truck has arrived! *By Fred Leavitt.*

A "general" store at the corner of 113th Street and St. Lawrence Avenue. *By Fred Leavitt.*

An important winter chore. *By Fred Leavitt.*

Dinner in the Hotel Florence dining room. *By Fred Leavitt.*

Pullman Wheelworks Apartments at the corner of Maryland Avenue and 104th Street. *Schoon.*

RESTORATION AND REJUVENATION

The Pullman Wheelworks Apartments building has had a variety of uses since it was built by the Pullman Company in 1918.[284] In 1919, fifty thousand phonograph cabinets were made here for the Edison Phonograph Works. From July 1920 to 1922, Pullman made about thirteen thousand steel automobile bodies for the Packard Motor Car Co.[285]

After being vacant for a number of years, the 294,000-square-foot building was remodeled in 1980, creating 210 attractive and affordable rental apartments including studios, one-, two- and three-bedroom units and a playground for children.[286]

THE GREENSTONE CHURCH[287]

There is a good reason that you can't find very many American buildings faced with Pennsylvania greenstone, known as serpentine stone. The rock is friable, meaning that it is fairly easily crumbled.

The church building could have been faced with Salem limestone found in southern Indiana and often simply called Indiana limestone. This popular

The Greenstone Church at the corner of St. Lawrence Avenue and 112th Street, December 2020. *Schoon.*

and durable building stone was used to build the National Cathedral in Washington, D.C., as well as the Pentagon and the Chicago's Board of Trade building. Back in 1880, architect S.S. Beman was acquainted with Indiana limestone, as many of the Pullman residences that he designed used Indiana limestone as accents. But this limestone is gray, and certainly greenstone makes a more dramatic view of the church—especially when seen among all the red brick buildings around it.

So greenstone was used, and it has for more than 140 years made his building one of the most-photographed buildings in the south Pullman neighborhood. But maintaining it has been an extra challenge for the congregation.

Since at least the 1950s, the congregation has had to concern itself with several renovation expenses. In 1954, the Chicago fire department notified the church trustees that the city might have to condemn the building.

Members were able to raise the $10,000 needed to make the necessary repairs through emergency fundraising, including the sale of "Greenstone bricks."[288] Although that crisis was averted, others have come up since then. But, although the congregation is and has always been rather small, nonmember residents of Pullman have often financially supported the 140-year-old church building.

OTHER GROUPS HAVE BEEN established as the need arose to support specific aspects of the community.

THE HISTORIC PULLMAN GARDEN CLUB[289]

The Garden Walk pamphlet, 2017. *Historic Pullman Garden Club.*

The Historic Pullman Garden Club has been an important part of the Pullman community since 1991, when three residents decided to form a club that would work toward beautification of the town. Club members maintain the circular beds in Arcade and Pullman Parks, Fulton Field and Gateway Gardens. They also sponsor several street corner beds, which are maintained by community residents.

The club hosts a number of events year-round (which is quite unusual for garden clubs). This includes its annual garden walk in June, an annual membership dinner, a reception every fall for Pullman house tour volunteers and a lecture series in the winter.

BIELENBERG HISTORIC PULLMAN HOUSE FOUNDATION AND THE PULLMAN HOUSE PROJECT

The Bielenberg Historic Pullman House Foundation is a nonprofit organization that is facilitating the restoration of a series of residential properties located in the historic town of Pullman so that the stories of the lives of the Pullman employees who lived there can be told. The foundation is named for David J. Bielenberg, the founding president of the Historic Pullman Foundation, who in his will established the foundation and donated to it his executive-style house.

The organization's goal is accomplished, in conjunction with the Historic Pullman Foundation, through the Pullman House Project, which is restoring selected Pullman housing units to the period (1881–1910) when the Pullman company owned and then rented housing to its employees. The goal is to eventually have one unit for each of the various housing units in the historical district. Docents at each house will tell the stories of Pullman workers and the families who lived there. Bielenberg's own house at 641 111th Street was the first unit to be showcased.

That house is used to tell the story of Thomas Dunbar and his family. Born in Scotland in 1864, Thomas Dunbar immigrated to Pullman in 1885, where he was employed as a carpenter. His family first lived in an apartment on Stephenson (now Champlain) Avenue. In 1896, when he was promoted to foreman, the family moved to a larger unit on Watt (now St. Lawrence) Avenue. In 1898, Thomas Dunbar was promoted to superintendent of the works, and the family moved into this house on Florence Boulevard (now 111th Street). He was later named vice president of the company. While volunteers have been restoring the house one room at a time, others have donated period furniture. The house is open for touring during the annual Pullman House Tour each October and by special arrangement

THE HOTEL FLORENCE

The Hotel Florence was in private hands from when the Pullman Company was forced to sell it until the 1970s. At first, business was great, so good in fact that in 1914 a four-story annex was built on the back of the hotel. But beginning with the Great Depression, and continuing after that, the number of guests at the hotel dwindled as orders for Pullman sleeping cars fell off.

Then when the company closed its shops in town and high-roller executives were no longer coming to the hotel, the rates were dropped, and the building became a boardinghouse and bar for the workers.

After years of losing money, the hotel closed. Uncared for, it was slated for demolition. To prevent that from happening, in 1975,[290] just days before

Hotel Florence, while being renovated in 2020. *Schoon.*

it was to be demolished, the hotel was purchased by the Historic Pullman Foundation, which then began restoration work and reopened the building for viewing while it temporarily operated the restaurant and considered what to do with the rest of the building

The Pullman State Historic Site

In 1991, the Illinois Historic Preservation Agency purchased the Hotel Florence and several Pullman Car Works buildings, including the Administration Clock Tower Building and the erecting shops on either side of it. Governor James Thompson, a Chicago native, liked the idea of using the buildings as a national railroad museum, one that would be the preeminent railroad museum in the country. "That's why we bought it," he once claimed.[291]

The state designated the combined area as the "Pullman State Historic Site." For a while, the Historic Pullman Foundation continued to operate the hotel restaurant while conducting tours and operating a museum on both the first and second floors. However, realizing that that restaurant management was not the main focus of the foundation, it turned management over to a private catering company.[292] That arrangement worked for a short time before the operation was shut down.

In 2000, the State of Illinois began a $3.2 million upgrade of the hotel's mechanical systems, roof and windows. It then began an aggressive renovation project in 2011 using funds provided by both public and private sources. This involved exterior work: a new roof, foundation repair and rebuilding and painting the veranda. Interior work included new lighting; restoring the kitchen, pocket doorways, oak floors and the grand staircase; renewing the lobby, the ladies' parlor and the billiard, reading and smoking rooms; restoring the hotel's stained glass; and installing an elevator.

THE CLOCK TOWER AND INDUSTRIAL BUILDINGS

As the workday was ending on Tuesday, December 1, 1998, Pullman residents saw that the iconic but empty Clock Tower Building and adjacent plant buildings were on fire. As is often the case with empty buildings, the fire had grown large before anyone realized the danger. The Chicago Fire Department was called to this five-alarm blaze (the most serious ranking), and 150 firefighters battled the fire until almost midnight.

A day or so afterward, a forty-five-year-old homeless man admitted to setting the blaze. Apparently, he had entered the building, set the fire and walked across the street to watch it burn. His family stated that he was mentally ill. At a trial the next year, he was found innocent by reason of insanity.[293]

Two days after the fire, the Pullman Civic Organization suggested that the state restore only the original Pullman buildings. The next several months were spent assessing the damage and deciding what should be repaired.

The support to restore the Clock Tower Administration Building and erecting shops grew first from the community's residents. In a short time, support was coming from other Chicagoans, from the broader Calumet area and from Illinoisans beyond Cook County to persons throughout the country, all recognizing Pullman's national significance.[294]

In April 1999, Illinois governor George Ryan named former governor Thompson to head a committee to investigate the possibility of rebuilding

The day after the fire: the devastated north erecting shops, the twentieth-century addition and clock tower. *Photo by Paul Petraitis; Petraitis collection.*

Clock Tower building being repaired, 2003. *National Park Service.*

the damaged buildings.[295] To help the state decide about restoring the building, a Clock Tower Campaign Committee was formed, and twenty thousand signatures were obtained on a petition urging the state to do the repairs.[296]

David Bahlman, then the executive director of the Landmarks Preservation Council of Illinois, emphasized that "Pullman is singularly unique and deserves the highest level of protection as a monument to the history of American industry." He named Pullman as one of the state's most endangered historic sites, stating that the clock tower was unique in that it was an industrial administration building but "resembled a town hall more than a factory."

In the spring of 1999, $3.4 million was allocated by the State of Illinois to stabilize the building, and in February 2000, Governor George Ryan authorized $10 million of Illinois FIRST funds to restore the clock and tower, repair the roof of the north erecting shop building and install new doors and windows and up-to-current-code electrical service.[297] Unfortunately, there was so much damage done to the south erecting shop that it was unable to be restored. It was razed, as was the adjacent 1908 addition.

Above and following three pages: The clock and new roof being set into place on the old Clock Tower, October 2005. *Photos by Paul Myers.*

Paul Myers remembered that on a crisp October day in 2005, when the new clock faces were hoisted up and attached to the tower, not surprisingly, a crowd had arrived to watch. However, not as expected, as the carefully executed effort was made to place the roof section on the very top, a southbound Metra train stopped on the tracks directly west of the building so that dozens of its passengers could peer out of the windows in order to witness this, for them, likely unexpected event.[298]

With no more money available to rehab the interior of the building and hopes for a railroad museum put on the back burner, the buildings sat empty for a few years as local groups wrote grant proposals to continue the repairs.

National Monument Designation

Of Chicago's fifty city landmark districts, the largest one is Pullman. And of those fifty, only Pullman has also been designated a state landmark and a national landmark. In addition, of those fifty districts, only Pullman is also a state historic site.[299]

By 2015, local Pullman organizations, the City of Chicago, local members of Congress, the governor of Illinois and scores of private citizens

President Barack Obama, signing the declaration that made Pullman a National Monument in the National Park Service. *White House Archives.*

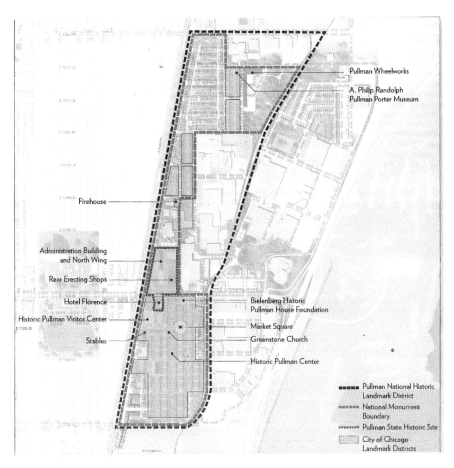

Labels on map:
Pullman Wheelworks
A. Philip Randolph Pullman Porter Museum
Firehouse
Administration Building and North Wing
Rear Erecting Shops
Hotel Florence
Historic Pullman Visitor Center
Stables
Bielenberg Historic Pullman House Foundation
Market Square
Greenstone Church
Historic Pullman Center

Pullman National Historic Landmark District
National Monument Boundary
Pullman State Historic Site
City of Chicago Landmark Districts

National Park Service.

recommended to the National Park Service and to President Barack Obama that the Pullman district become a National Monument (a designation similar to a National Park). That year, following research conducted by the National Park Service and the donation by the Illinois Historic Preservation Agency of the Administration Clock Tower Building, President Barack Obama came to Chicago and, at the Gwendolyn Brooks College Preparatory Academy (previously the Pullman Manual Training School), formally declared Pullman a National Monument.

As expected, National Monument designation has brought new interest in the Pullman area and almost immediately allowed for greater opportunities to tell the story of this unique American neighborhood.

ARTSPACE LOFTS

For years, Pullman has been a haven for artists and that only increased after the national monument designation. The block on the east side of Langley Avenue, between 111th and 112th Streets, is now the site of a three-building complex for artists and their families. It consists of a new building with twenty-six apartment units, built in 2019 and specifically designed to reflect the nineteenth-century buildings in the town. That building is bookended with two smaller original historic Pullman apartment buildings that stood empty for years but have since been rehabbed and the exteriors restored. These two buildings are the original blockhouses "A" and "C," which now have six units each. The complex includes a two-thousand-square-foot gallery where the residents can exhibit their work. Residents are also invited to hang their finished projects in the hallways.

This housing project was developed through a partnership of Chicago Neighborhood Initiatives, Pullman Arts and Artspace, a national organization dedicated to creating, fostering and preserving affordable and sustainable spaces for artists and arts organizations.

ArtsSpace Lofts. *Schoon.*

FINALLY

Finally, in the middle of the 2020 COVID-19 pandemic, enough funding was acquired through numerous grants and private donations that work could commence on major projects, including comprehensive site development work of the car works site that includes mitigation of contaminated soil, installation of underground utilities, landscaping including rebuilding the workers' gate on 111th Street, the famous PULLMAN sign made of Indiana limestone letters and its decorative stone wall and interpretive exhibits. Also being built are a driveway, parking lot and maintenance facility. A ceremonial groundbreaking was held on Labor Day 2020 to celebrate the beginning of this major effort to ready the facility for visitors.

THE SIGNIFICANCE OF PULLMAN

Understanding the history of the town of Pullman helps one better understand American history. The town started out as a thoroughly integrated planned industrial community, but life in this town did not become what was expected by those who designed it.

Pullman is the site of the largest if not the first completely planned major industrial town in the United States. From its earliest days, it was described as a "model" town—a town that could be emulated elsewhere.

The Pullman Company revolutionized rail travel, becoming a name associated with comfort, luxury and impeccable service. The company, by providing comfortable travel experiences, spurred tourism through this country and Canada.

The company's refusal to negotiate working conditions and salaries with its employees led to a strike and widespread boycott that had national ramifications, the least of which was the designation of the first Monday in September as Labor Day.

The Pullman companies hired formerly enslaved men and women when many other companies wouldn't. For decades, the Pullman Company employed more African American workers than any other company in the United States.[300]

The Pullman Company was the first large American corporation to sign a labor agreement with an African American union. The hiring of thousands of Black men as porters, and the ultimate success of the Brotherhood of Sleeping Car Porters negotiations, helped build the Black middle class. The organizing skills developed by the Brotherhood Porters led to many of the successes of the civil rights movement in the mid-twentieth century.

The residential sections of the town of Pullman are largely intact today. Its visual continuity, meticulously planned in the 1880s, is still obvious even to casual visitors. The lessons learned through Pullman's labor/management negotiations are still valuable. It was at Pullman that American manufacturers realized that they could not and should not ignore employee grievances.

The citizens of Pullman have shown the nation the power of community cooperation.

At Pullman, many of its buildings, no longer being used for their original purpose, have been restored and repurposed. In Pullman's becoming a city, state and national landmark, and then a national monument, the lessons learned there can more readily be told to others.

Pullman was designed to be a model industrial town. It then became a "model" national monument. That description can be applied, as it was named a national monument at the request of its residents and local organizations as well as by elected city, state and federal officials. The National Park Service was invited to be a part of the community, and it has done so through partnerships with local organizations such as the Pullman Civic Organization and the Historic Pullman Foundation as well as with the city and state governments. In 2021, the Historic Pullman Foundation became an official "friends" group of the National Park Service. All these groups work together toward common goals.

Appendix

THE PULLMAN BUILDING DOWNTOWN

I n 1883, during a break in building of the town of Pullman, George Pullman asked S.S. Beman to design an office building for him to be built right on Michigan Avenue in downtown Chicago

For his building, a lot on the corner of Adams Street and Michigan Avenue, right across the street from the Art Institute, was purchased. Beman's design for the impressive ten-story office building included red granite, brick and terra cotta with a corner turret and other decorations on the top.

The building, at 79 East Adams Street, was described by the *Chicago Tribune* as one which gave "an expression of dignified elegance in its simple massiveness." Being designed just a decade after the devastating Chicago Fire, the stone building with iron beams and stairways was advertised as being "absolutely fireproof." It had five elevators, one for freight and four for passengers, and both gas and electric lighting.

The ground floor was made available for retail stores; the second and third floors were reserved for Pullman company offices. Rentable office spaces occupied the fourth through sixth floors. Beman's own architectural offices were probably on the fifth. A multiuse building, the seventh, eighth and ninth floors were used for bachelor and small family apartments, each with running water and a private bathroom, but probably in a reaction to the fire, no cooking was allowed in them. There was a restaurant or tearoom on the ninth floor, while the kitchen and staff apartments were located on the top floor. The basement had laundry facilities and electric light generators. The offices and residential units had separate entrances and elevators.

The Pullman Building on Chicago's Michigan Avenue. *Petraitis collection.*

Although two Chicago telephone companies were renting space in the building, the Michigan Avenue reception area had an old-fashioned speaking tube that allowed an attendant to call the apartments to determine if the occupants happened to be at home.

The building was lighted with 2,200 sixteen-candlepower Edison lamps powered by a generator in the basement. The elevators were hydraulic—they rose or fell upon a tug on a rope. Thus, the top floor, with the best views, was not used for the president of the corporation but for service staff instead.

All the rented spaces, including the private apartments, were maintained by the Pullman company service staff.

NOTES

1. Pullman's Geologic Beginnings

1. Schoon, Calumet Beginnings.

2. The Railroad Era Begins

2. Porterfield, *Dining by Rail*, 5.
3. Buder, *Pullman*, 6.
4. Porterfield, *Dining by Rail*, 5.
5. Buder, *Pullman*, 6.
6. Ibid.
7. Ibid.
8. Ibid.
9. Porterfield, *Dining by Rail*, 5.
10. Ibid., 9.
11. Ibid., 12.
12. Ibid., 29.
13. Ibid., 30.
14. Ibid., 31.

3. George Pullman in New York

15. Leyendecker, *Palace Car Prince*, 13.
16. Ibid., 16–17.
17. Leyendecker, *Palace Car Prince*, 13.
18. Theobald, "Field & Pullman."
19. Leyendecker, *Palace Car Prince*, 21.
20. Ibid., 24.
21. Buder, *Pullman*, 5.
22. Ibid., 7.
23. Ibid.
24. Ibid., 37.
25. Leyendecker, *Palace Car Prince*, 36.
26. Ibid., 26.
27. Ibid.
28. Buder, *Pullman*, 4.

4. Raising Chicago and Pullman's First Sleepers

29. Leyendecker, *Palace Car Prince*, 29.
30. Ibid., 33.
31. *Chicago Daily Tribune*, Friday, July 26, 1861, http://www.nike-of-samothrace.net/csc.html.
32. Leyendecker, *Palace Car Prince*, 36.
33. Schnell, "Sez You."
34. Theobald, "Field & Pullman."
35. Ibid.
36. Leyendecker, *Palace Car Prince*, 41.

5. Gold Fever

37. Ibid., 46.
38. Ibid., 46–47.
39. Ibid., 51.
40. Ibid., 57.
41. Ibid., 64.
42. Ibid., 61.

43. Ibid., 63.
44. Dictionary of Unitarian & Universalist Biography, "George Pullman."

6. Improving the Sleeper Car

45. Leyendecker, *Palace Car Prince*, 75.
46. Pullman State Historic Site, "Pullman Company."
47. Buder, *Pullman*, 10.
48. Ibid.
49. Ibid.
50. Leyendecker, *Palace Car Prince*, 79.
51. Ibid.
52. Ibid., 78.
53. Buder, *Pullman*, 12.
54. Leyendecker, *Palace Car Prince*, 38.
55. Theobald, "Field & Pullman."
56. Porterfield, *Dining by Rail*, 41.
57. Ibid., 41–42.
58. Ibid.
59. Leyendecker, *Palace Car Prince*, 81.
60. Theobald, "Field & Pullman."

7. The Pullman Palace Car Company

61. Leyendecker, *Palace Car Prince*, 87; Theobald, "Field & Pullman."
62. Leyendecker, *Palace Car Prince*, 87.
63. Ibid., 88–89.
64. Ibid., 90.
65. Ibid., 88.
66. Pullman State Historic Site, "Pullman Company."
67. Buder, *Pullman*, 14.
68. Carnegie, *How to Win Friends*, 82–83.
69. Pullman State Historic Site, "Pullman Company."
70. Carnegie, *How to Win Friends*, 82–83.
71. Dictionary of Unitarian & Universalist Biography, "George Pullman."
72. Leyendecker, *Palace Car Prince*, 109.
73. Ibid., 111.

74. Ibid., 112.

75. Buder, *Pullman*, 19.

76. Leyendecker, *Palace Car Prince*, 111.

77. Pullman State Historic Site, "George Mortimer Pullman; Pinterest, "Driehaus Museum."

78. Pullman State Historic Site, "George Mortimer Pullman."

79. Beberdick and the Historic Pullman Foundation [hereafter HPF], *Chicago's Historic Pullman District*.

80. Buder, *Pullman*, 32–33.

81. Scarlett and Walton, *Archaeological Overview & Assessment*, 16.

82. Leyendecker, *Palace Car Prince*, 161–62.

8. Pullman Porters and Maids

83. Ibid.

84. Chateauvert, *Marching Together*, 23.

85. Leyendecker, *Palace Car Prince*, 203; Carwardine, *Pullman Strike*, 20

86. Leyendecker, *Palace Car Prince*, 203.

87. National Park Service [hereafter NPS], *Foundation Document*, 10.

88. Duncan, "Pullman Porters."

89. Chateauvert, *Marching Together*, 22.

90. Ibid.

91. Ibid., 27.

92. *Chicago Defender*, December 31, 1910.

93. Chateauvert, *Marching Together*, 27.

94. World Heritage Encyclopedia, "Pullman Porters."

95. Chateauvert, *Marching Together*, 27.

96. Ibid., 24.

9. West of Lake Calumet Before Pullman

97. Scarlett and Walton, *Archaeological Overview & Assessment*, 14.

98. Rowlands, "Down an Indian Trail."

99. Van Hinte, "Netherlanders in America," 346.

100. Andreas, *History of Chicago*, 607.

101. Encyclopedia of Chicago, "Kensington."

102. Scarlett and Walton, *Archaeological Overview & Assessment*, 36.

10. Pullman: Industrial and Commercial Assets

103. Ibid., 19.
104. Ibid., 18.
105. Ibid., 39.
106. Vogel, "Introduction," in Carwardine, *Pullman Strike*, x.
107. Leyendecker, *Palace Car Prince*, 167.
108. Scarlett and Walton, *Archaeological Overview & Assessment*, 39.
109. Ibid.
110. Ely, "Pullman."
111. NPS, *Foundation Document, Pullman National Monument,* June 2017, 5.
112. Beberdick and HPF, *Chicago's Historic Pullman District*, 8.
113. Pullman State Historic Site, "Town of Pullman."
114. Petraitis, personal communication, December 28, 2020.
115. NPS, *Foundation Document,* 12.
116. Scarlett and Walton, *Archaeological Overview & Assessment*, 36.
117. Chicago Public Library, Historic Pullman Collection.
118. Pullman State Historic Site, "Town of Pullman."
119. Pullman State Historic Site, "Planning the Town."
120. Leavitt and Miller, *Pullman*, 10.
121. Chicago Public Library, Historic Pullman Collection.
122. Buder, *Pullman*, 70–71.
123. NPS, *Pullman Historic District Reconnaissance Survey*, 24.
124. Pullman State Historic Site, "Famous Pullman Band."
125. NPS, *Pullman Historic District Reconnaissance Survey*, 24.
126. Ely, "Pullman."
127. Scarlett and Walton, *Archaeological Overview & Assessment*, 44.
128. Pullman State Historic Site, "Town of Pullman."
129. Scarlett and Walton, *Archaeological Overview & Assessment*, 39.
130. Ibid., 36.
131. Ibid., 39.
132. Schnell, "Sez You."
133. Leyendecker, *Palace Car Prince*, 167.
134. *Pullman Journal* (Fall–Winter 1981–82), 4.
135. Historic Pullman Foundation, "1881 Description of the Hotel Florence."
136. *Pullman Journal* (Fall–Winter 1981–82), 4.
137. Historic Pullman Foundation, "1881 Description of the Hotel Florence."
138. Ibid.

139. Historic Pullman Foundation, "Hotel Florence."
140. Ibid.
141. Petraitis, personal communication.
142. Carwardine, *Pullman Strike*, 20. The date of the *Chicago Evening Post* was not given.
143. NPS, *Pullman Historic District Reconnaissance Survey*, 23.
144. Doty, *Town of Pullman*, 14.
145. Ely, "Pullman."
146. Carwardine, *Pullman Strike*, 16–17.
147. Buder, *Pullman*, 63.
148. Ibid., 64.
149. Corcoran, "Pullman Library."
150. Bey, "State Grant to Restore Market Hall."
151. Pullman State Historic Site, "Pullman Timeline."
152. Leavitt and Miller, *Pullman*.
153. Leyendecker, *Palace Car Prince*, 169.
154. Black and Smith, "History."
155. Wolski, "Pullman Clock Tower Fire Remembered," privately printed flier.
156. Carwardine, *Pullman Strike*, 20.
157. Bey, "Before History Vanishes."
158. Grand Royal Arch Chapter of the State of Illinois, "Former Temples."
159. Ely, "Pullman."
160. Wolski, "Pullman Clock Tower Fire Remembered."
161. Ibid.
162. Carwardine, *Pullman Strike*, 19.

11. Pullman: Residences and Early Residents

163. Scarlett and Walton, *Archaeological Overview & Assessment*, 37.
164. NPS, *Foundation Document*, 6.
165. Wolski, "Pullman Clock Tower Fire Remembered."
166. NPS, *Foundation Document*, 6.
167. Pullman State Historic Site, "Town of Pullman."
168. Ibid.
169. *NPS, Foundation Document*, 11.
170. Ely, "Pullman."
171. Carwardine, *Pullman Strike*, 22.
172. Ibid., 19.

173. Beberdick and HPF, *Chicago's Historic Pullman District*, 39.
174. NPS, *Foundation Document*, 6.
175. Hirsch, *After the Strike*, 13.
176. NPS, *Foundation Document*, 10
177. Pullman State Historic Site.
178. Doty, *Town of Pullman*, 25.
179. Source for text and photos: Pullman State Historic Site, http://www.pullman-museum.org.
180. Doty, *Town of Pullman*, 5.
181. Vogel, "Introduction," in Carwardine, *Pullman Strike*, xii.
182. Leyendecker, *Palace Car Prince*, 165.
183. Higinbotham, *Report of the President*, 8.
184. Pullman State Historic Site.
185. History Reader, "Railroads, the Chicago World's Fair, and George Pullman."

12. Unrest, Annexation and Strike

186. Ely, "Pullman."
187. Leyendecker, *Palace Car Prince*, 181.
188. Buder, *Pullman*, 199.
189. Ibid.
190. *Chicago Tribune*, September 21, 1888.
191. Vogel, "Introduction," in Carwardine, *Pullman Strike*, x.
192. Buder, *Pullman*, 112.
193. Scarlett and Walton, *Archaeological Overview & Assessment*, 38.
194. Ibid., 38.
195. Leyendecker, *Palace Car Prince*, 220.
196. Carwardine, *Pullman Strike*, 23.
197. Leyendecker, *Palace Car Prince*, 221–22.
198. Ibid., 222.
199. NPS, *Foundation Document*, 7.
200. Leyendecker, *Palace Car Prince*, 223.
201. Carwardine, *Pullman Strike*, 35.
202. Vogel, "Introduction," in Carwardine, *Pullman Strike*, xlii.
203. Bey, "State Grant to Restore Market Hall."
204. Leavitt and Miller, *Pullman*.
205. Leyendecker, *Palace Car Prince*, 226.

206. Carwardine, *Pullman Strike*, 38.
207. Ibid., 16.
208. U.S. House of Representatives, "First Labor Day."
209. Ibid.
210. NPS, *Foundation Document*, 7.
211. Kelly, *Edge of Anarchy*, 143.
212. Ibid., 146.
213. Illinois Labor History Society.
214. Leyendecker, *Palace Car Prince*, 226.
215. Kelly, *Edge of Anarchy*, 154.
216. Leyendecker, *Palace Car Prince*, 226.
217. Carwardine, *Pullman Strike*, 39.
218. Ibid.
219. Leyendecker, *Palace Car Prince*, 226.
220. Ibid., 227.

13. Repercussions

221. Ibid., 229.
222. NPS, *Foundation Document*, 9.
223. Vogel, "Introduction," in Carwardine, *Pullman Strike*, xxxiii.
224. Ibid., xxxiv.
225. Leyendecker, *Palace Car Prince*, 254.
226. Ibid., 258.
227. Ibid.
228. Pullman State Historic Site, "Pullman Company."
229. Beberdick and HPF, *Chicago's Historic Pullman District*, 114.

14. Pullman Porters Organize

230. Doty, *Town of Pullman*, 57.
231. Misra, "Town That Laid the Foundation."
232. Chateauvert, *Marching Together*, 68.
233. Shmoop Editorial Team, "History of Labor Unions."
234. National Railroad Museum, "Help Create a Labor Union."
235. NPS, *Foundation Document*, 10.
236. Chateauvert, *Marching Together*, 53.

237. Ibid., 2.
238. Ibid., 3.
239. Ibid., 54.
240. Salter, "Brotherhood of Sleeping Car Porters."
241. Chateauvert, *Marching Together*, 69.
242. NPS, *Foundation Document*, 2017.
243. Fleming, *Pullman Porters*, 333.
244. Chateauvert, *Marching Together*, 16.
245. Ibid., 165.
246. Biography.com, "E.D. Nixon."
247. AFL-CIO, "A. Philip Randolph."

15. The Pullman Company and the Town 1897–1945

248. Biography.com, "Robert Todd Lincoln."
249. www.Pullman-Car.Com.
250. Kelly, *Edge of Anarchy*, 268.
251. NPS, *Foundation Document*, 9.
252. Chicago Public Library, Historic Pullman Collection.
253. History Matters, "Digest of Jim-Crow Laws."
254. Pullman State Historic Site, "Filling in Lake Vista."
255. Pullman State Historic Site, "Pullman Company."
256. Simons and Parker, *Railroads of Indiana*, 50.
257. Encyclopedia of Chicago, "Zoning."
258. Bundles, "Up from the Sleeper Car."
259. Leavitt and Miller, *Pullman*, 13.
260. Mid-Continent Railway Museum, "Haskell & Barker."
261. Ibid.
262. Theobald, "Field & Pullman."
263. Chicago Public Library, "About Pullman Branch."
264. Ibid.
265. Alton, "I Remember Roseland."
266. Howat, *Standard History*, 300.
267. Federal Writers' Project, Calumet Region Historical Guide.
268. Brunner, "Pullman Standard."

16. The Postwar Years

269. Pullman State Historic Site, "Pullman Timeline."
270. Ibid.
271. Encyclopedia of Chicago, "Hammond, IN."
272. Ibata, "Ryerson Buys Part of Pullman Plant."
273. Amtrak, "'Somethin' Special'."
274. Ibid.
275. UtahRails, "Amtrak Superliner Cars."

17. Citizen Involvement and Pride, Restoration and Recognition

276. Petraitis, "Pullman Civic Organization."
277. Ibid.
278. Leavitt and Miller, *Pullman*.
279. Ibid.
280. Pullman State Historic Site, Façade Legacy Project.
281. Scarlett and Walton, *Archaeological Overview & Assessment*, 20.
282. Leavitt and Miller, *Pullman*, 14.
283. Pullman History Site, Friends of the Florence Fundraiser Brochures.
284. NPS, "Historic Pullman Wheelworks."
285. Pullman State Historic Site, "Pullman Timeline."
286. Mercy Housing, "Pullman Wheelworks Apartments."
287. Pullman State Historic Site, "Pullman Timeline."
288. Ibid.
289. Ibid.
290. Historic Pullman Foundation, Hotel Florence.
291. Thompson, interview.
292. Deardorff, "Pullman Ends Ties to Restaurant."
293. Mellen, "Ryan Releases Pullman Repair Funds."
294. Wolski, Personal conversations.
295. Pullman State Historic Site, "Pullman Timeline."
296. Wolski, "Pullman Clock Tower Fire Remembered."
297. Mellen, "Ryan Releases Pullman Repair Funds."
298. Myers, "Fall Day in Pullman," unpublished paper digitized by the Pullman History Site.
299. artspace, Pullman Artspace Lofts.
300 NPS, Foundation Document, 10.

BIBLIOGRAPHY

Printed Material

Alton, Andrea Moore. "I Remember Roseland." *Where the Trails Cross* 29, no. 4 (Summer 1999).

Andreas, A.T. *History of Chicago from the Earliest Period to the Present Time.* Vols. 1–3. Chicago: AT Andreas, 1884.

Beberdick, Frank, and the Historic Pullman Foundation. *Chicago's Historic Pullman District.* Charleston, SC: Arcadia Publishing, 1998.

Bey, Lee. "Before History Vanishes." *Chicago Sun-Times*, April 12, 1999.

———. "State Grant to Restore Market Hall." *Chicago Sun-Times*, September 3, 2000.

Black, Frank, revised by Reverend Bill Smith. "A History of the Pullman United Methodist Church." Undated, unpublished pamphlet available on the Pullman History Site: https://www.pullman-museum.org/pshs/pshsCompoundObjectWebPage.php?collection=pshs&pointer=19954&root=19958.

Bretz, J. Harlen. *Geology of the Chicago Region.* Urbana: Illinois State Geological Survey, 1939.

Buder, Stanley. *Pullman: An Experiment in Industrial Order and Community Planning, 1880–1930.* New York: Oxford University Press, 1967.

Bundles, A'Lelia. "Up from the Sleeper Car." *New York Times*, July 25, 2004.

Carnegie, Dale. *How to Win Friends and Influence People.* New York: Simon & Schuster, 1936.

Carwardine, William H. *The Pullman Strike.* Chicago: Charles H. Kerr & Company, 1973.

Chateauvert, Melinda. *Marching Together: Women of the Brotherhood of Sleeping Car Porters.* Vol. 314. Champaign: University of Illinois Press, 1997.

Chicago Defender. December 31, 1910.

Chicago Tribune. September 21, 1888.

D'Alessio, F.N. "Fire Wrecks Last Chicago Pullman Plant Building." *Detroit Free Press,* December 8, 1998.

Deardorff, Julie. "Pullman Ends Ties to Restaurant." *Chicago Tribune,* nd. https://www.pullman-museum.org/pshs/pshsFullRecord.php?collection =pshs&pointer=13900.

Doty, Mrs. Duane. *The Town of Pullman: Its Growth with Brief Accounts of Its Industries.* Chicago: TP Struhsacker, 1893.

Ely, Richard T. "Pullman: A Social Study." *Harper's New Monthly Magazine,* February 1885.

Federal Writers' Project. *The Calumet Region Historical Guide.* Gary, IN: Garman Printing Company, 1939.

Fleming, G. James. "Pullman Porters Win Pot of Gold." *Crisis* 10 (1937).

Grant, H. Roger. *Railroads and the American people.* Bloomington: Indiana University Press, 2012.

Harper, Charlton, E. *Railway Car Builders of the United States & Canada.* New York: Interurban Press, 1957.

Higinbotham, Harlow Niles. *Report of the President to the Board of Directors of the World's Columbian Exposition: Chicago, 1892–1893.* Chicago: Rand, McNally & Company, 1898.

Hirsch, Susan E. *After the Strike: A Century of Labor Struggle at Pullman.* Vol. 314. Lincoln: University of Nebraska Press, 2003.

Howat, William F. *A Standard History of Lake County, Indiana, and the Calumet Region.* Chicago: Lewis Publishing Company, 1915.

Ibata, David. "Ryerson Buys Part of Pullman Plant." *Chicago Tribune,* February 16, 1987.

Kelly, Jack. *The Edge of Anarchy: The Railroad Barons, the Gilded Age, and the Greatest Labor Uprising in America.* New York: St. Martin's Press, 2019.

Leavitt, Fred, and Nancy Miller. *Pullman, Portrait of a Landmark Community: A Photographic Essay.* Chicago: Historic Pullman Foundation, 1981.

Leyendecker, Liston Edgington. *Palace Car Prince: A Biography of George Mortimer Pullman.* Niwot: University Press of Colorado, 1992.

Mellen, Karen. "Ryan Releases Pullman Repair Funds." Unidentified newspaper, February 24, 2000. https://www.pullman-museum.org/pshs/pshsFullRecord.php?collection=pshs&pointer=15633.

Mitchell, Patricia B. *Dining Cars and Depots*. Chatham, VA: self-published, 1992.

Mitchell, S. Augustus, Jr. *Mitchell's New General Atlas*. Philadelphia: S. Augustus Mitchell Jr., 1865.

Myers, Paul. "A Fall Day in Pullman." https://www.pullman-museum.org/pshs/pshsCompoundObjectWebPage.php?collection=pshs&pointer=19446&root=19448.

National Park Service. *Foundation Document, Pullman National Monument*. Chicago, 2017.

———. *Pullman Historic District Reconnaissance Survey*. Chicago, 2013.

Porterfield, James D. *Dining by Rail: The History and Recipes of America's Golden Age of Railroad Cuisine*. New York: Macmillan, 1998.

Rotzall, Brenda Warner. "Grant Approved for Pullman Site." *Chicago Sun-Times*, January 25, 2001.

Rowlands, Marie K. "Down an Indian Trail: The Story of Roseland." *Calumet Index*, 1949.

Scarlett, Timothy J., and Steen A. Walton. *Archaeological Overview & Assessment: Pullman National Historical Monument*. Lincoln, NE: Midwest Archaeological Center, National Park Service, 2017.

Schoon, Kenneth J. *Calumet Beginnings: Ancient Shorelines and Settlements at the South End of Lake Michigan*. Niwot: Indiana University Press, 2003.

Simons, Richard S., and Francis Haywood Parker. *Railroads of Indiana*. Bloomington: Indiana University Press, 1997.

Struzi, Diane. "Pullman Efforts Picking up Steam." *Chicago Tribune*, December 14, 1998.

Van Hinte, Jacob. "Netherlanders in America: A Study of Emigration and Settlement in the 19th and 20th Centuries in the United States of America." *Journal of American Ethnic History* 5, no. 2 (1986).

Vogel, Virgil J. "Introduction." In *The Pullman Strike*, by William H. Carwardine. Chicago: Charles H. Kerr & Company, 1973.

Wolski, Michael. "Pullman Clock Tower Fire Remembered—One Year Later." https://www.pullman-museum.org/pshs/pshsFullRecord.php?collection=pshs&pointer=16039.

Wright, Helena E. "George Pullman and the Allen Paper Car Wheel." *Technology and Culture* 33, no. 4 (1992): 757–68.

Nonprint Sources

AFL-CIO. "A. Philip Randolph." https://aflcio.org/about/history/labor-history-people/asa-philip-randolph.

Amtrak. "'Somethin' Special': A Superliner History." https://history.amtrak.com/blogs/blog/creating-somethin-special-a-short-history-of-the-superliners.

artspace. "Pullman Artspace Lofts." https://www.artspace.org/pullman.

Biography.com. "E.D. Nixon." https://www.biography.com/activist/ed-nixon.

————. "Robert Todd Lincoln." https://www.biography.com/people/robert-todd-lincoln-20989843.

Brunner, Amy. "Pullman Standard." Butler County Historical. https://butlerhistorical.org/items/show/29.

Chicago Public Library. "About Pullman Branch." https://www.chipublib.org/about-pullman-branch.

————. Historic Pullman Collection. https://www.chipublib.org/fa-historic-pullman-collection/.

Citylab. https://www.bloomberg.com/citylab.

Corcoran, Kate. "The Pullman Library." https://www.pullman-museum.org/theTown/pullmanLibrary.html.

Dictionary of Unitarian & Universalist Biography. "George Pullman." https://uudb.org/articles/georgemortimerpullman.html.

Duncan, Jordan. "Pullman Porters, America's First Black Union." https://afram101autumn2015.wordpress.com/2015/12/12/pullman-porters-americas-first-black-union-2.

Encyclopedia of Chicago. "Hammond, IN." http://www.encyclopedia.chicagohistory.org/pages/562.html.

Grand Royal Arch Chapter of the State of Illinois. "Former Temples." http://ram-il.org/chapters/former-temples.

Historic Pullman Foundation. "An 1881 Description of the Hotel Florence." http://www.pullmanil.org/hotel_1881article.htm.

————. "The Hotel Florence." http://www.pullmanil.org/hotelflorence.htm.

History Matters. "Digest of Jim-Crow Laws Affecting Passengers in Interstate Travel." http://historymatters.gmu.edu/d/6327.

The History Reader. "Railroads, the Chicago World's Fair, and George Pullman." https://www.thehistoryreader.com/us-history/railroads-chicago-worlds-fair-george-pullman.

Illinois Labor History Society. http://www.illinoislaborhistory.org.

Interview with James Thompson. https://presidentlincoln.illinois.gov/ Resources/52d7d633-5f2e-4d63-9b26-a7dd4cb6deee/Thompson_Jam_ PFNL_Vol_IV.pdf.

Mercy Housing. "Pullman Wheelworks Apartments." https://www. mercyhousing.org/lakefront/pullman-wheelworks-apartments.

Mid-Continent Railway Museum. "Haskell & Barker." https://www. midcontinent.org/rollingstock/builders/haskellbarker.htm.

Misra, Tanvi. "The Town That Laid the Foundation for America's Civil Rights Movement." CityLab, https://www.bloomberg.com/news/ articles/2015-02-19/the-town-that-laid-the-foundation-for-america-s-civil-rights-movement.

Myers, Paul. Personal conversations, January 2021.

National Park Service. "Historic Pullman Wheelworks." https://www.nps. gov/places/historic-pullman-wheelworks.htm?utm_source=place&utm_ medium=website&utm_campaign=experience_more&utm_ content=small.

———. "The Pullman Story, Part 2." https://www.nps.gov/pull/learn/ historyculture/the-pullman-story-part-2.htm?fullweb=1.

National Railroad Museum. "Post Visit Activity: Help Create a Labor Union." https://fh-sites.imgix.net/sites/2564/2019/04/23153718/ post-visit-help-create-a-labor-union.pdf.

Petraitis, Paul. Personal conversations, December 2020–January 2021.

———. "The Pullman Civic Organization." http://www.pullmancivic.org.

Pinterest, "Driehaus Museum." https://www.pinterest.com/pin/53269146 2147930835/?lp=true.

Preservation Chicago. https://preservationchicago.org/chicago07/ pullman-historic-district.

Pullman-Car. "Welcome Aboard the *Abraham Lincoln*." www.Pullman-Car.com.

Pullman State Historic Site. Façade Legacy Project. https://www.pullman-museum.org/facades.

———. "The Famous Pullman Band." http://www.pullman-museum.org/ thePeople/thePullmanBand.html.

———. "Filling in Lake Vista." https://www.pullman-museum.org/pshs/ pshsFullRecord.php?collection=pshs&pointer=15173.

———. Friends of the Florence Fundraiser Brochure. https://www. pullman-museum.org/pshs/pshsFullRecord.php?collection=pshs&point er=16874.

———. "George Mortimer Pullman." http://www.pullman-museum.org/theMan.

———. "Planning the Town." http://www.pullman-museum.org/theTown/planning.html.

———. "The Pullman Company." https://www.pullman-museum.org/theCompany.

———. *Pullman Journal* (Fall–Winter 1981–82), 4, https://www.pullman-museum.org/pshs/pshsCompoundObjectWebPage.php?collection=pshs&pointer=20994&root=20997.

———. "The Town of Pullman." http://www.pullman-museum.org/theTown.

Salter, Daren. "Brotherhood of Sleeping Car Porters (1925–1978)." BlackPast. https://www.blackpast.org/african-american-history/brotherhood-sleeping-car-porters-1925-1978.

Schnell, Hans B. "Sez You - - Sez I." Pullman History Site. https://www.pullman-museum.org/pshs/pshsFullRecord.php?collection=pshs&pointer=16107.

Shmoop Editorial Team. "History of Labor Unions Introduction." https://www.shmoop.com/history-labor-unions/.

Theobald, Mark. "Field & Pullman, Pullman's Palace Car Co., Pullman Co., Pullman Inc., Pullman-Standard Mfg. Co. Pullman-Standard Co." Coachbuilt. www.coachbuilt.com/bui/p/pullman/pullman.htm.

Unitarian Universalist History and Heritage Society. https://uudb.org/articles/georgemortimerpullman.html.

U.S. House of Representatives. "The First Labor Day." https://history.house.gov/Historical-Highlights/1851-1900/The-first-Labor-Day.

UtahRails. "Amtrak Superliner Cars." https://utahrails.net/pass/amtrak-superliner-cars.php.

Wolski, Mike. Personal conversations, December 2020–January 2021.

World Heritage Encyclopedia. "Pullman Porters." http://www.self.gutenberg.org/articles/Pullman_porters.

INDEX

V

Vanderbilt, Commodore Cornelius
    40, 41

W

Wagner Car Company 40, 41, 113
waterworks and drainage 59
west of Lake Calumet before
        Pullman 48, 54
  Kensington 50
  Roseland 50
Wheelabrator-Frye, Inc. 138
Williams, Benzette 56, 59
women
  as maids 45, 106
  as passengers 17
  as shop workers 106
  in the shops 131
  not permitted to register 68
  supporting the Brotherhood 109
Women's Economic Councils 109
World's Columbian Exposition 73,
        86, 92, 93
  Pullman displays 89

ABOUT THE AUTHOR

Ken Schoon, a Northwest Indiana native, is a professor emeritus at Indiana University Northwest, where he taught for more than forty years. He is the author of half a dozen books about the history of the greater Chicago/Northwest Indiana area, including *Calumet Beginnings: Ancient Shorelines and Settlements at the South End of Lake Michigan*, *Dreams of Duneland* and *Shifting Sands: The Restoration of the Calumet Area*. Most, to some extent, note the relationship between the geology of the area and its human history. He is a founding board member, past president and advisor to the Dunes Learning Center, a member of the Advisory Council of the Shirley Heinze Land Trust, and a member of the Indiana Historical Society, which gave him the Dorothy Riker Hoosier Historian Award in 2016. In 2019, he received the Dunes Learning Center's Green Apple Award for Environmental Education Excellence.

Visit us at
www.historypress.com
··